ALL ABOUT THE BENJAMINS:

Helping People Create Sustainable Wealth In the Midst of Financial Insanity

MELANIE DENISE PERRY

SANKOFA PRESS
P.O. BOX 125
LOS ANGELES, CA 90043
877.907.2282

Published by:
Sankofa Press
P.O. Box 125
Los Angeles, CA 90043

All rights reserved. No part of this publication may be reproduced, stored in a retrieval system, or transmitted in any form or by any means, electronic or mechanical, including photocopying, recording or otherwise, without the prior written permission from Sankofa Press except for the inclusion of brief quotations in a review.

This publication is designed to provide accurate and authoritative information in regard to the subject matter covered. It is sold with the understanding that neither the author nor the publisher is engaged in rendering legal or accounting services. If legal advice or other expert assistance is required, the services of a competent professional person should be sought.

Dip account™ and Zeallionaire(s)™ are trademarks of Melanie Perry. The contents of this book are protected by copyright and trademark laws under U.S. and international law. All rights reserved.

From a Declaration of Principles jointly adopted by a Committee of the American Bar Association and a Committee of Publishers

First Edition.
© 2010 by Melanie D. Perry
Cover photo by Albert Neal

ISBN: 978-0-578-06875-6

Library of Congress Control Number: 2010914934

Printed in the United States of America

This book is printed on acid free paper.

I dedicate this book to future generations: my cousin Kennedy Ferguson and to my nieces, Brianna and Annelise Murray.

Gratitude

I am grateful to God for planting and nurturing this seed to develop and grow into what I have become. I am grateful to my parents, Melville and Rosalind Perry, for their guidance, support and exposure to God. I give thanks to my sister, Erica Murray, for her encouraging words and listening ear. To my friends and associates, Crysti and Tellis Bethel, Albert Neal, Luva Robinson Vera, Lanette Ware-Bushfield, Clarence Zanders, Yausmenda Ali-Bay, Barbara Herzer, Steve Light, Cindy Ashton, Reginald Scurlock, Kahshanna Evens and Dawn Santos for their confidence in me with manifesting this book, which helped to keep me going when trials crossed my path. I am very appreciative of my uncle Johnny Mills and aunt Janice Stephens for their unconditional support and for creating space for me to make this book a reality. To my business coaches, Sheila Reed and Stephanie Ardrey, for keeping me focused and providing sound advice on strategic planning in my financial planning practice and other social entrepreneurial endeavors. I appreciate the direction and insight provided by one of my editors, Janice R. Littlejohn. I would be remiss if I did not mention Rev. Leslie White and Rev. Najuma Smith for being my mentors and instrumental at bringing financial literacy to the community. I give thanks to my colleagues, Ryan Myers, Justin Chee, Anthony Beltran, Paul Adams, Marguerite Rangel, Andrea Schaffer, Jamila Haseeb, Erin Coovert, Warren Hoppe, Gerald Lee and Rick Bell for being a sounding board and/or the voice of inspiration. I am obliged to everyone at Pacific Advisors, Guardian and Park Avenue Securities who contributed to the regulatory *requirements necessary to complete this book. I must mention Malia Whitenack and especially Don Leider who where integral in helping me navigate through the agency compliance/legal department for content approval. And finally, I appreciate Kelly Kidwell, president and CEO and Neil Willner, Managing Partner of Pacific Advisors, for having the vision and the fortitude to bring forth a financial services firm infused with a philosophy of care throughout the agency. I am blessed to be surrounded by greatness and be able to live out my God given purpose.*

Contents

Foreword ix

Introduction xi

Chapter One 1
    The New Spiritually Grounded Millionaire

Chapter Two 9
    Does Your DNA Generate Wealth?

Chapter Three 13
    It Happened Before and It Will Happen Again

Chapter Four 21
    A Nation Reborn

Chapter Five 29
    The Making of a Zeallionaire

Chapter Six 35
    The Development of Generational Zeallionaires

Chapter Seven 41

Becoming a Zeallionaire

Chapter Eight..47
Plan for Abundance

Chapter Nine 73
Motivational Guide

Special Acknowledgement...79

About the Author 81

Appendix..83

Foreword

Melanie Perry has prepared a valuable financial guide, aimed at educating a population lacking in financial knowledge. The approach is direct and easy to both understand and digest. This guide is filled with historical nuggets to not only provide a foundation, but to additionally provide the "why" as to the importance of having financial education. Each chapter provides a building block for readers to glean insights which are applicable immediately in their wealth building plans—irrespective of how well developed those plans are. To your wealth!

Stephanie Ardrey
MAOM, President/CEO, ArdreyGroup LLC

West African Symbol of Unity and Human Relations

Introduction

Is there any sense to be made from the financial insanity we face on a personal, national and global level? Is it possible to make sense of it all and in the process create wealth? I am not just talking about material wealth, but physical, mental and, most important, spiritual wealth. Though it may seem like a tall order, it is possible to create sustainable wealth in the midst of financial insanity and remain true to self.

It all begins in the mind. Our Creator has given us the gift of choice. By choosing to focus on the positive aspects of our life experiences we can more readily learn from our mistakes and treasure our blessings. This reminds me of a book by Herman J. Clemons Sr. called *You Are What You Think All Day Long*. The mind is the source of creativity, including the creation of sustainable wealth. The ability to express our creativity, skills and talents and to use those resources despite current circumstances is based on internal knowledge. Having a solid understanding of our unique skills and gifts is critical to developing them and sharing them with the world. However, only a few of us know how to transform understanding into knowledge and knowledge into wisdom and therefore create sustainable wealth. Wisdom, embraced by God, combined with an action plan and tenacity can defuse external circumstances and thus help create sustainable wealth despite current circumstances.

The three stages to gaining wealth are knowledge, planning and tenacity. In order to attain wealth it is imperative we accomplish these stages simultaneously. A person that knows no better can do no better. This is true for society as well. In order to shift paradigms, there needs to be a common understanding. Then and only then can change occur. As new habits formulate around this new understanding, knowledge is gained. Through development of this knowledge, wisdom is born. This book assumes an understanding of the need to learn about money in a truly different way. It advocates for a yearning to develop habits that allow us to live a life of abundance. Moreover, the book demands we create ways to sustain wealth throughout our lives and over generations.

Knowledge, the first stage towards attainment of wealth, is also the key component to creating sustainable wealth. The source of this power is within our control. First we must make the decision to acquire knowledge in seven key areas: knowledge of our creator and of our selves, our communities, both locally and globally, general and specialized knowledge to create niches in particular markets.

The second stage to creating sustainable wealth necessitates having a well thought out and flexible plan to address our current circumstances and future outcomes. Life is full of bumps and bruises. How well we navigate our way around the tough times can make a difference at how much we appreciate the good times.

When the economy is in flux, it is difficult to tell where we are headed financially. There is a natural tendency to sell an investment at a loss and run for cover. However, if we have a solid strategic plan and our cash flow, assets, liabilities and asset protection are properly balanced, volatile market conditions will have less of an effect on our current and future financial well-being. The objective is to have a clear plan. This plan should ensure we get to our intended results and address basic needs first. Secondly, the plan should account for life's luxuries. And, finally, this plan should be flexible; it should provide a framework or a blue print that allows adjustment during challenging times and harvesting in times of abundance.

The third stage toward sustainable wealth is the journey itself. Tenacity, will-power, drive, steadfastness and persistence are critical characteristics of this stage. All the knowledge in the world combined with a master plan means nothing if there is no fuel for take off. Numerous wonderful ideas, inventions and master plans lay dormant in the minds of brilliant people. When no action is taken, a gift dies with its inventor.

Action transforms these ideas, inventions and master plans into the modern conveniences we benefit from and enjoy today including radio, television and the Internet. These technologies manifested because their investors remained steadfast until their ideas, inventions or master plans became concrete realities. It cannot be stressed enough how integral it is to activate the plan and stay the course. It should come as no surprise that this stage towards achieving sustainable wealth is the most difficult of the three. The difficulty is inherent in the fears we face when called upon to share our skills and talents with the world. Fear can eat us alive or, if we allow it, motivate us to action. Why haven't we taken positive action towards answering God's calling? Could it be that our friends and family may not support our ideas? Are our ideas so big that once attained they will broaden our exposure to the extent certain folks will be left behind? This may be the time in our lives when it is necessary to expand our circles or create new ones. We must affirm that we are worth it, that we have the ability to achieve our goals. Upon acceptance of these affirmations, we should keep it moving.

These three stages of creating sustainable wealth can provide comfort in the midst of insanity as we learn and understand that we have a degree of control over the outcome. Another comforting note is that as long as we have the ability to create and use the resources around us, the negative impact of current circumstances have little effect on who we are or what we are capable of becoming. We have been through enough to know we can handle any storm we may face as we embark on the journey towards sustainable wealth.

West African Symbol for Change

Chapter One
The New Spiritually Grounded Millionaire

Today's economically empowered consists of a group of spiritually-grounded, well-informed individuals. They are the new "social" entrepreneurs. These people create products and services using God-given talents to bring added value to humanity. This group understands the value and usefulness of traditional and co-operative economics, the very essence of capitalism. This is a Zeallionaire, one that knows their God-given purpose, skills and talents. They use them to benefit humanity while creating personal monetary wealth. When we view capitalism through a spiritual lens, we become aware that there are basic principles that are in alignment with God's promise of abundance for all, should we choose to seek it. Our Creator has provided all that we need for anything we have been called upon to do in our lives—the underlining assumption is that there is something within us all that is unique to us as individuals. So many of us wonder what exactly is our purpose in life. If you are on a quest to find your life's purpose, then research ways to find your unique gift.[1] If you have found your

---

[1] Warren, Rick. *Purpose Driven Life*. Zondervan. Michigan, 2007; Beckwith, Michael Bernard. *Spiritual Liberation: Fulfilling Your Soul's Potential*. Atria. New York. 2008; D'Annunzio, Steve. *Prosperity Paradigm*. Mercury Print. New York. 2006. The previous books are great resources to get you on your path.

life's purpose, take action and use capitalism to help you *monetize*[2] your skills and talents.

The purpose of our being is to share our unique skills and abilities, whatever these things may be, as long as they bring added value. Capitalism allows us the opportunity to translate our talents into monetary gain. We do not have to sell our soul to achieve financial wealth. There are many ways to monetize our unique gifts with integrity. Millions of people seek specialized education to find niches where our skills and talents can be most beneficial. Thousands of people get degrees and certifications in such fields as information or computer technologies, software programming, employment services, management consulting, science and technology, home health care, personal financial advising, child care services, art, entertainment, recreation and motion pictures.[3] The idea is to use capitalism to enhance our well being and bring added values to others. Capitalism is not an evil system. It depends on how the economic system is used. Consider real estate, for instance. When business negotiations are both, ethical and genuine, for both the seller and the buyer, real estate can be a viable wealth building asset. When real estate is not used in its highest and best use, it can lead to financial ruin personally and globally as we experienced in the Great Recession of 2008. Eco-friendly businesses and careers can also build wealth and simultaneously help improve our environment. If we step up to the plate and live purposeful lives, then collectively we can make changes for the benefit of humanity. This creates a win-win situation. No one has to lose if people begin to collaborate instead of compete. In many ways, the basic premise of our economic system was designed to be in align-

---

2 Monetize is the conversion of tangible and intangible assets into money.
3 *Top 10 Industries.* 2009. <www.Inc.com>

ment with our God-given rights and purposes. The forefathers of our nation were very much aware of this truism and set out to outline the Declaration of Independence, a fundamental set of human rights based on these truths. They keenly understood the liberties and capabilities of humans. The essence of the declaration proposes that all people should be able to exercise the right to explore their life's purpose.

Many of us are happiest when we are doing the things we love to do. When we have found our life's purpose, we can find a job, career or business in an industry that we enjoy. When we engage in activity we enjoy there is a tendency to do it well. This, in turn, activates the laws of attraction,[4] which can lead to various levels of wealth. This is what God has in store for us. Our Creator is all about abundance, not scarcity. There are enough resources to provide a home, food and clothing for everyone. What we must remember is that God is our source and the systems humans have created, like capitalism, can be used for the greater good.

Capitalism, at its finest, gives people the opportunity to use their unique gifts and resources to benefit society.

The very essence of capitalism allows someone from humble beginnings to share their talents with the world for a medium of exchange (money). The Founding Fathers were in tune with the intentions of the Creator and thus developed a nation that allows people to benefit from their God-given inalienable rights. Since the dawn of this nation, we have witnessed countless examples of individuals that found their purpose by identifying a need, a personal interest or recognizing a talent within that activated the laws of attraction. They attracted the right people, found themselves in the right

---

[4] The Law of Attraction is a universal law that signifies like attracts like and that our thoughts manifest our reality due to direct conscious focused attention.

places and had access to the resources necessary to expand on their ideas.

Fred DeLuca[5] started from humble beginnings. Initially, he thought his God-given purpose was to become a doctor but he lacked the funds to finance his education. A friend suggested DeLuca open a sandwich shop as a means to pay for college. This sandwich shop eventually expanded into a chain of Subway stores. After many lessons learned, DeLuca grew the Subway stores at an accelerated pace. Persistence was a critical factor in DeLuca's formula for success. A belief in his abilities, access to the right resources and alignment with people who believed in him helped DeLuca start Subway, the world's most popular sandwich shop[6].

Elena Medo,[7] an inventor and business owner, started her first company after experiencing challenges breast feeding her third child. Medo invented a breast pump that was more accommodating to her particular needs. The pump became so popular that she decided to start a business. As Medo learned more about the breast milk industry, it became clear to her that there was a need to make improvements. Her clarity of purpose opened up doors that allowed her to take a leap of faith. Medo founded Prolacta, the first and only commercially available human milk fortifier for critically ill and premature babies.

Reginald Lewis,[8] a businessman, attorney, author, and philanthropist was born to a working class family. During his

---

5 Evan Carmichael. *The Sandwich King: The Early Years of Subway's Fred DeLuca.* [cited 2010]. <http://www.evancarmichael.com/Famous-Entrepreneurs/2095/summary.php>
6 Entrepreneur named Subway the #1 franchise in 2010. [cited 2010] <www.Subway.com>
7 The San Diego Tribune. Land of Milk and Honey. [updated Feb. 19 2006, cited 2008]. <http://www.signonsandiego.com/uniontrib/20060212/news_lz1n12milk.html >
8 Nancy Rivera Brooks. TLC Beatrice International. [updated Jan. 20 1993. Cited 2008]. <http://articles.latimes.com/1993-01-20/business/fi-1542_1_leveraged-buyout>

youth he was known for his drive and thirst for excellence. It was this undeniable belief in self that led him to the path of success. Drive helped Lewis recognize opportunities that led him to become a savvy businessman. Lewis' God-given talents were developed on the playing field, in the classroom and in the boardroom. He never allowed the idea of a glass ceiling hinder him from pursuing his goals. It is said that he relied on moxie, financial and legal savvy, to negotiate his deals. His clarity of purpose allowed the laws of attraction to work in his favor. In 1987, Lewis purchased Beatrice International. This purchase was the largest international leverage buyout in American history.

Each of these individuals had special skills and talents that were fine tuned through the acquisition of specialized knowledge. Each person experienced success by remaining steadfast until the intended results of his or her business venture was accomplished.

For every positive, naturally, there is a negative. Capitalism at its worst can be a rather diabolical system. Corruption, however, can only prevail when it is allowed or when the powerless are helpless to react or respond. Various aspects of the fast food industry are examples of the negative results of capitalism. *Fast Food Nation*, a film released in 2006, forever changed the fast food industry by revealing the adverse effects of consuming trans fatty acids, chemicals and artificial flavors. This is a perfect example of the benefits of gaining power through knowledge, having specialized knowledge and using our skills, talents and resources to create awareness and effect change. In light of the health food revolution, fast food restaurants and snack food companies are making efforts to improve the ingredients in foods. The consciousness of Americans is rising to new heights. The people mentioned above have brought added value to humanity, whether through creating a healthy product that is low in calories and high in nutrition, providing nutritional milk to nurse premature and sick babies or through philanthropy. Contributing their skills, talents and abilities along with effective use of their personal resources has made a deep impact on society. The phrase, "the last shall be first and the first shall be last"[9], is worth noting. It is our time to bring forth our greatness and monetize our skills and talents. In a capitalistic world our skills should not only pay the bills, but also afford us the promises of God. Seek out what we love to do and discover the various ways to create an abundant life. Convert your skills and talents into multiple streams of income. In addition to the previously mentioned entrepreneurs, there are many others worth studying including the following:

- Madam C.J. Walker, entrepreneur and inventor of Madam Walker's Wonderful Hair Grower

- Tyler Perry, multi talented writer/producer/director/actor

- Tom Anderson, creator of MySpace.com

- Jerry Yang, co creator of Yahoo.com

- Rachael Ray, host of a cooking television show

- Elon Musk, creator of Pay Pal and XSpace

- Deepak Chopra, MD and author

---

[9] The Disciple Matthew. *The Bible*, Matthew 20:16

- Jennifer Lopez, multi-talented entertainer

- Ed Mercer, philanthropist and real-estate developer

The common thread among these successful, enlightened people is that they all acquired a specialized knowledge in an area they enjoyed. Monetizing our skills and talents does not mean that we have to compromise our integrity. We can create wealth by developing our skills and talents in a way that benefits humanity. Read other people's success stories for motivation. The time is ours—and the time is NOW.

West African Symbol for Humility Together with Strength

Chapter Two
Does Your DNA Generate Wealth?

Epictetus, a Greek philosopher, asserted "God has entrusted me with myself." The philosopher's assertion helps to address the question does our DNA generate wealth? To further understand the depth of this question we must gain a clear understanding of DNA. Deoxyribonucleic Acid (DNA) is the brain of every cell that makes up the entire body. It can recreate itself and contains vital information that gets passed down to each generation. There are 75-100 trillion cells in our bodies. Given the right conditions and fed the right information our DNA can develop into something new.

So how do we know if our DNA can result in our becoming a Zeallionaire™? Does one have to go through a process to change the cellular structure of her or his DNA? Consider the following questions:

1. Do I want wellness, financial abundance and healthy relationships?

2. Am I willing to take the necessary steps to create abundance and prosperity in multiple ways?

3. Am I willing to power through the tough times, learn from *failures* and work collaboratively in order to see my idea of abundance come to fruition?

4. Do I feel worthy enough to share my skills and talents with humanity?

5. Do I feel humanity is worth it?

If we answered "yes" to the above questions, then our DNA is equipped with the right information to help us become Zeallionaires with a degree of ease. All that is necessary is that we allow the essence of our being to come forth. If we have answered "no" to some of the questions, then we may be in a gestation period and additional emotional and spiritual work must be done.

Zeallionaires are confident, yet humble beings because they have a sincere sense of self. The main driving forces behind Zeallionaires are self-worth and self-confidence. These are key DNA strands that are integrated in the physical forms of all Zeallionaires. At the core of our being we have to feel that we are worth having abundance. We have to know that we are worthy of good health, financial wealth, and empowering relationships. These are our inalienable rights. Confidence is necessary to express the talents given to us by God. Only we can express our God-given talents; no one can do this for us.

If I am one that has been oppressed socially or otherwise, I must find my voice and feed it with new liberating thoughts that come from education. I need to surround myself with people of like mind. I cannot settle for mediocre ideas or entertain the company of mediocre people if I intend to claim this magnificent change in my life.

These are times of great change. It is time for an awakening of our talents so that we may bring forth great change for the betterment of humanity. We must allow our DNA to generate wealth in every form.

Some of us may be asking, what characteristics or strands of DNA lead to wealth? The underlining characteristics of Zeallionaires are that they are confident, focused, courageous, detail-oriented and fearless. They consider *failures* as lessons that provide clarity for the next move. They are amenable to seeking help. They are prepared when opportunity comes and they have strong networks. If we have the previously mentioned characteristics, then our DNA can generate wealth. If we realize that we need to work on a few of these characteristics and we are proactive at making these improvements, then our DNA can generate wealth.

The following are a few resources to help restructure our DNA:[10]

1. Identify where there is lack and limitation. Meditate, pray and read. Cindy Ashton facilitates meditation on her CD, *Kiss the Monster Meditations: The Courage to be Successful*; Deepak Chopra and Iyanla Vanzant have a series of books to help change our DNA. *The Seven Spiritual Laws of*

---

[10] These publications and websites have not been reviewed or approved by PAS. PAS does not recommend or endorses them in any way." Links to other sites are for your convenience in locating related information and services. This Agency, Park Avenue Securities, LLC (PAS) and their representative do not maintain these other sites and have no control over the organizations that maintain the sites or the information, products or services these organizations provide. This Agency and PAS cannot guarantee their completeness or suitability for and purpose. Accordingly, this Agency and PAS expressly disclaim any responsibility for the content, the accuracy of the information or the quality of products or services provided by the organizations that maintain these sites. This Agency and PAS do not recommend or endorse these organizations or their products or services in any way.

Success and *The Higher Self* by Chopra and *One Day My Soul Just Opened Up* by Vanzant are good starts. The *Bible, Koran, Torah* and other sacred texts are excellent reads as well.

2. Feed the brain with relevant data. *Think and Grow Rich: The Black Choice* by Napoleon Hill and Dennis Kimbro, *The Success Principles* by Jack Canfield, *The Millionaire Next Door* by Thomas J. Stanley and William D. Danko are books that are great food for the brain.

3. Create a healthy environment. Visit www.AlGore.com as well as www.ConsciencousLivingTV.com and incorporate environmentally friendly products and habits into your daily life. You can also visit www.Intent.com to find a community of people with similar goals to create a support system.

4. Create a clutter-free lifestyle of proactive behavior. Clutter can keep us at a stand still. Remove clutter from the home, office, car and mind. *Getting Things Done* by David Allen can provide fresh ideas and direction.

5. To completely modify an old pattern, a new paradigm must be reinforced for a minimum of 52 days. It takes 22 days to break a habit and the next 30 days to create the new pattern as a habit.[11] Establish a routine to address each one of these areas. In due time, these habits will effect a great change in your life. We are truly in the midst of an economic revolution of greatness. Be ready to be a part of it.

---

[11] D'Annunzio, Steve. *Purpose Driven Life*. Mercury Print. New York. 2006.

West African Symbol for "He that does not know, can know from learning"

Chapter Three
It Happened Before and It Will Happen Again

"Those that do not learn from history are doomed to repeat it."[12] The crash of 2008 was a result of deregulating legislation that was established as early as the 1940s. From 1940 to around 2001, changes in securities law created an environment for Wall Street to engage in practices that were outlawed to help prevent our current economic crisis. Imagine you are in your ninth grade financial literacy class. Your teacher is educating the class on the following events that led to the crash of 1929. Life was looking pretty good for many Americans. The First World War was far behind. Americans took pleasure in a new invention called the radio. Although there was a great disparity between the rich and the poor, cars were becoming more affordable, which allowed more people to enjoy one of life's pleasures. And, in the financial world, the stock market was at an all time high. Between 1924 and 1929, the Dow Jones Industrial Average quadrupled; it was the longest bull market ever. Until this time no one had ever seen such a booming market mainly because the Dow Jones Industrial Average wasn't created until 1894. Many people thought the bull market would

---
12 George Santayana is an American philosopher, poet and humanist.

last forever, which helped to lure more investors. A new concept called installment plans allowed more people to buy products and houses as well as invest on margin, a form of credit in the investment world. People borrowed money to invest in the real estate and stock markets. By September 1929, steel production was down, several banks had failed and fewer homes were built, yet no one paid attention to these clear indications that an economic shift was happening in the business world despite the fact that the Dow increased 27% from the previous year. By October 23, 1929, the financial bubble began to burst and by November 13, 1929, the market finally bottomed out.[13]

Does any of this sound familiar? Imagine if this relevant economic history was studied in all of our schools versus only a few. If more Americans had financial literacy courses in junior high or high school, then current day American society would have been better equipped to recognize this bull market will at some point shift to a bear market. What goes up will eventually come down. Financial literacy is critical to helping us make better decisions about our money. And, if it was required by all states for both public and private schools, the average American would have greater financial security.

Knowing U.S. economic history will not only help us make smarter choices with our money, it will help us to be more aware of legislation that has a direct impact on our financial well being. So, when legislation like the Commodities Future Modernization Act of 2000 arises the people of America will have a stronger voice and therefore challenge such damaging acts. It was this act and many others that resulted in a series of deregulations in the securities industry that opened up the door for Wall Street to run wild. Most of the bills passed right

---

13 Claire Suddath. Brief History of The Crash of 1929. [updated Oct 29, 2008, cited 2008] <www.time.com/time/nation/article/0,8599,1854569,00.html>

under the nose of Congress. It was assumed Wall Street could handle its own affairs. Little did some Congress members know that the legislation to register derivatives and credit default swaps would lead to financial mayhem. Knowing our history is imperative. Credit default swaps are a revised version of the bucket shops in the early 1900s. If financial literacy was as common as math and English in our school system, then perhaps more members of Congress would have seen the foreshadowing events of this inevitable financial debacle.

Educating ourselves on financial matters is critical beyond measure. We need to know more than how to pick a stock or a mutual fund. We must educate ourselves politically as well. We have to hold our political officials accountable for any financial misdeeds. But first we have to hold ourselves accountable so we can make informed voting decisions. In addition, having a broad perspective of a subject matter and understanding the past and the present, can help develop a level of knowledge that can put us in a better position in the future. History provides us with the wisdom needed to reveal signs in the present that can gravely impact our futures.

Until recently, many of us thought that the stock market crash of 1929 was the most devastating economic crisis the United States had ever seen. However, if we were to look back in time, we would discover that the depression that followed the crash of 1929 was not the first but actually the fifth major depression in the history of the United States. There were at least 13 recessions[14] since the 1800s. About every three years we go through an economic cycle. Ebbs and flows occur continuously. What is important is that we get comfortable with the fact that the economic cycles, expansions, prosperity, contraction, and scarcity are a part of the business eco-

---

14 http://thehistorybox.com/ny_city/panics/panics_article16a.html

nomic cycle. This is no different than the ebbs and flows of our own lives. How often do we find ourselves reaping the harvest then suddenly finding ourselves in the middle of a financial storm? We can see the same cycles in nature. The four seasons directly correlate to the four business cycles. Spring represents growth and expansion, summer represents the peak of the harvest, fall represents a decline in growth and winter represents stagnation and receding. The business cycle is a fundamental concept of economics, something we should have learned and fully understood in secondary school. Knowledge is the fundamental difference between the haves and have nots.

The commentary in the media is that this economic crisis is unprecedented due to its global impact. While the effects are grand, this is not the first time Americans, and thus the modern world, has experienced such devastating economic turmoil on a global scale. The abolishment of the global slave trade in the early 1800s marked the beginning of a multitude of unprecedented economic crisis. In 1840, cotton was the most valuable export of all the U.S. exports combined. Twenty years later, the value of slave property was greater than the value of all the American railroads, banks and manufacturing. The global impact of OPEC and America's dependence on oil is comparable to the global and economic impact of cotton in the late 1800s. The South produced about $7/8$ of the world's cotton.[15] When the New World and the rest of the Western Hemisphere gradually adopted the Emancipation Proclamation from 1804 to 1888, the world had to make a major shift in its dependence on slaves and slave labor as a commodity. When major shifts and transitions occur, they may be hap-

---

15 Meltzer, Milton. *The Cotton Gin*. New York, Benchmark Books Marshall Cavendish, 2004.

pening because something better is trying to emerge. How many of us have sat on a business idea or invention that could have benefited humanity? The human experience is about how well we cope with the ebbs and flows we encounter in our lifetime and what lessons we learn. In this global shift of change, acting on our ideas now could be pivotal to creating sustainable personal wealth and effecting a beneficial change in society.

Again, market fluctuations are natural ebbs and flows of the business cycle. The catalyst that moves this cycle is greed and fear. Greed is what has gotten us into this current economic debacle. The media tends to feed our fears and evoke panic. Certainly there is reason to be concerned and aware. However, we know that chaotic events of this degree have occurred previously in the United States and globally. The events should inform us on how to handle our personal finances in each phase of the economic cycle. Knowledge of events that led to recessions in the past will help us make better financial decisions, especially when we take notice of particular signs. Consider the various "bucket shops" of the early 1900s. Bucket shops were places where people placed side bets on whether a stock would go up or down, all without purchasing the stock.[16] Congress took immediate action and passed a law making this side activity illegal. Our law makers realized this side activity manipulated the stock market. The "bucket shops" led to the panic and ultimate recession in 1907. Then, about 100 years later, Congress passed a bill called the Commodities Futures Modernization Act of 2000, which allowed the concept of "bucket shops" to reemerge in the form of Credit Default Swaps. This law gave Wall Street

---

16 If you recognized this concept as an option contact, you're right. However, options are legal and regulated.

immunity from state gambling laws and legalized activity that had been banned for most of the 20th century.[17]

Take note. The financial industry, including the former Federal Reserve Chairman Alan Greenspan, encouraged Congress to pass the bill that was endorsed by former President Bill Clinton. The bill was based on the notion that the financial industry could do it better than the government.[18] The Federal Reserve, "an independent entity within the government, having both a public purpose and private aspects"[19], lowered interest rates to record levels as a means to encourage spending. The flip side was that more and more people were able and willing to buy big ticket items like houses and cars because they could borrow money dirt cheap. Bringing more people to the marketplace in this instance pushed up prices and activated an emotional reaction, which increased prices even more. This created a strong demand for a product that was full of air, which caused the highly inflated housing prices of the early 2000s. The prices were not justified based on old-school economic principles. We can clearly see now that when this goes on for too long a volcano erupts worldwide. The passing of this bill created a frenzy from Wall Street to Main Street. This low interest environment combined with relaxed lending requirements opened up the door to a vast majority of people with no real financial means to support large purchases. This created a floodgate with sub-prime lending and borrowing. New products were created using securitiza-

---

17 Steve Kroft. The Bet That Blew Up Wall Street. [Updated Aug. 2009, cited 2009]. <http://www.cbsnews.com/ stories/2008/10/26/60minutes/main4546199_page2.shtml>
18 Same reference in footnote 17.
19 *History of the Federal Reserve.* [cited 2008] <www.federalreserveeducation.org/FRED/faq/faq.cfm>

tion[20] practices developing mortgage backed securities that bundled these sub-prime mortgages. To encourage investors to buy these securities, insurance was required and credit default swaps began to emerge. These mortgage backed securities, backed by credit default swaps and derivatives, were sold on Wall Street through some hedge fund investment companies as well as institutional and private investors worldwide. The bases of these swaps were essentially a bet on whether or not the people would pay their mortgages. People of limited means and limited financial knowledge were the largest group encouraged to acquire the largest investment that most Americans buy only once in a lifetime. Greed was clearly one of the driving forces that put the U.S. and world economy into a tailspin.

Hindsight is always 20/20. While we may not have been able to predict this crisis, knowing the fundamentals of economics and a degree of financial history would have given us warning signs that something was not kosher. This knowledge could assist us in making sound financial decisions. The person that held the knowledge had the key to the Emerald City. If basic financial literacy courses are not required curriculum, then we are setting our children up to experience the same financial setbacks we are dealing with today. A basic level of understanding about money could have calmed emotions and allowed pragmatic financial decisions to be the driving force as opposed to panic. Mathematicians and economists alike provide theories and formulas to support these emotions and behaviors and attempt to forecast the future. Knowing the fundamentals is a major factor in creating sustainable wealth. Enroll in a financial literacy course or workshop today.

---

20 Securitization is a structured finance process, which involves pooling and repackaging of cash flow producing financial assets into securities that are then sold to investors. Available at <www.merage.uci.edu>

West African Symbol for the importance of wisdom and learning from the past in building the future

Chapter Four
A Nation Reborn

A spiritual revival is steadily emerging in America; the world as we know it is changing. This is evident as we look at major events over the past decade with a wide-angled view. What is revealed is a great deal of pain and suffering. By the end of 2001, Americans experienced the following events:

- The dot com boom and eventual bust

- September 11, 2001, terrorist attacks

- Embezzlement cases of CEO's from Worldcom and Enron

- Pursuit of Osama Bin Ladin

- The search for "weapons of mass destruction" and eventual war with Iraq and Afghanistan

- Former President Bush's response to the victims of Hurricane Katrina

- Scientific revelations of the major causes of global warming[21]

- Deregulating on Wall Street, which led to the worst recession in decades

Yet, in the center of this havoc, there is an emergence of goodness that rises to the top. The pendulum is shifting towards a more positive view of humanity. More marketers angled (especially in commercials for life insurance) campaigns on helping others. Other ad campaigns emphasized control over our kitchens and the amount of television watched. A popular billboard read "Not in my kitchen, I make the rules". A television commercial aired during children's programs suggested going out to play versus watching television. Burger restaurants have stepped up and are providing healthier options on their menus. Millions of Americans are making money via the Internet and, in turn, spreading the wealth by providing added resources that help people enhance their lifestyles. All of this is done with a giving mentality versus one of scarcity, lack and limitation. Thousands came to the aid of Hurricane Katrina victims as it became apparent that our government would not provide adequate rescue measurements. A former senator of Illinois chose to answer the call and, against all odds, stepped out on faith and ran for president. The mere fact that, President Barack Obama won the candidacy by a land slide and that the entire world was tuned

---

21 Interview with George Monbiot. *The World Is a Bit of a Time Bomb.* [updated Oct 2008; cited 2008]. <www.pbs.org/wgbh/pages/frontline/heat/etc/world-co2.html>

in, is a clear indication that the pendulum is shifting towards a collective mindset of a "we" versus "me" society. A new day is dawning.

The interesting thing about rebirth is that more often than not we have to go through chaos, confusion, uncertainty, challenges and even pain in order for a new beginning to emerge. Dr. Michael Bernard Beckwith, Senior Minister of Agape International Spiritual Center, mentioned in one of his sermons in 2009 that challenging times do not always call for a bail out because something new may be trying to emerge.[22] Bailing out would only hinder or prevent that particular development that could be of great benefit to that individual and/or the world. It is common to think great atrocities like earthquakes, tsunamis and world hunger are so devastating that nothing good can come out of them. However, many new inventions, new beginnings and new ways of doing things can come from challenging situations. For example, the Green Belt movement, founded by Wangari Maathai, PhD, was born out of devastating environmental conditions as a result of deforestation in Kenya. Maatahi discovered that a solution to the soil runoff, water pollution, difficulty finding firewood, and lack of animal nutrition was to plant a tree. There were only 9 trees planted for every 100 trees cut. Over time the Green Belt movement made a significant difference in the lives of Kenyans. This success did not come without a great deal of trial and tribulation. There were countless challenges with the Kenyan government as well as educating the people on the impact a simple tree could make in improving the conditions of their lives. As a result of all of Maatha's personal triumphs and the Green Belt movement, she not only won the

---

22 Michael Bernard Beckwith. *Spiritual Liberation: Fulfilling Your Soul's Potential.* Artia. New York. 2008

Nobel peace prize[23] but she has made a tremendous impact on humanity. The life of Wangari Maathai is an excellent example of a Zeallionaire allowing greatness to emerge from a very difficult set of circumstances. In terms of the most recent economic crisis, many lessons were learned and a shift towards positive new beginnings is happening now.

Despite how horrific our financial crisis is, we have to shift our thinking and look at our current national and personal financial crisis as an opportunity to clean out and start anew. This is the rough part of the journey that does have an ending. If we are able to gain wisdom from this crisis, our outcomes will be much better than the ones where no wisdom was gained. Life brings about ebbs and flows. The key is to keep getting up when we are knocked down.

Historically, in times of crisis, whether it is on a personal level or in business, new ideas and inventions are conceived to provide a solution or to address new and existing needs. Understand clearly that we are in the midst of a revolutionary change; to be exact, we are facing an economic revolution of greatness.

Throughout the journey, whether it is on a personal, national or international level, one has to ask the question as Marvin Gaye did in 1971, "What's Going On?" Specifically, What in the world is going on? Analyzing the events that have occurred over this decade may make some people wonder, "How can this be a revolution of greatness?" These events look like signs leading to the end of the world. Well, I am not a psychic. However, I would argue that it is more of the end of an age versus the end of the world. Reverend Coco Stewart, a minister at Agape International Spiritual Center, suggested

---

23 Kenyan Ecologist Win Nobel Prize. [updated Oct. 2004; cited 2009]. <http://news.bbc.co.uk/2/hi/africa/ 3726024.stm>

in one of her sermons that the pandemonium we have seen so far in this decade is actually answered prayer. That surely sounds ludicrous, some might say. But think about it for a minute. List three major events that took place in your own life and analyze the journey. It can almost be guaranteed that there was at least one event in that journey that was heartbreaking, confusing, uncertain, chaotic, painful, worrisome and possibly depressing or disappointing. Yet when we look at the end results, we see that the experience and insight we gained was worth the painful journey. We have to be still, look for the positive in all of our experiences and know that all of our needs are met. There are resources surrounding us ready to assist us in reaching our dreams. In the words of Mahatma Gandhi, "Be the change you want to see."

Christopher Gardner, investor and author of the *Pursuit of Happiness*, endured a great deal of hardships on the road to happiness. After separating from his wife, both he and his son lived in motels, shelters, slept on the floors of public bathrooms, skipped meals, rode the bus and then, finally, got an apartment. At one point he offered to paint the apartment building in exchange for rent. All the while, Gardner studied for an intense stock broker exam, participated in the training and sold bone density scanners to make ends meet. Mr. Gardner had his eye on the prize. And where there is a will there is a way. Despite the circumstances Gardner faced, he had an undeniable belief in self to stay the course. In reflection, Gardner said that he would not trade anything for the journey. Success is achieved by first believing in self, fine tuning our skills, taking action and defining failure as learning lessons. In light of personal circumstances and the problems our nation is facing, there is light at the end of the tunnel. In order to get to the end of the tunnel we have to go through a purging process and get rid of the habits and people that do not propel us to the next level. Once you have exfoliated all that dead skin, the new you can come forward and share your skills and talents with the world.

Based on what we have seen so far in the 21st century, we are well overdue for a thorough detox. The question we must ask is, "What is God trying to bring out of humanity? What is God trying to emerge through us in this new age?" We know for certain that Barack Obama is one person that was to emerge in this new era. A need for environmentally sound products and services is another. YOU are the final variable to the equation. What have you been called to do that you have not moved on yet? Just think what the world would be like if the Wright brothers had not created the first functional air craft or if Henry Ford had not engineered the Model T, if Amos E. Joel, Jr. had not invented a device that sparked the cell phone industry.[24] What if Patricia Bath had not created the "Laserphaco Probe"[25] making cataract surgery more accurate and more comfortable for the patient? The world would not be this far developed in world-wide travel. Transportation and communication would not be at the click of a button and some people would be unnecessarily blind. "If not you, then who? And, if not now, then when?"

Knowledge comes in all forms, formal and informal. It is up to us to seize the opportunity when it knocks on our doors. As our knowledge transforms into wisdom, pass it on. It is so essential to pass on the knowledge as a means not to recreate the wheel. Be a mentor to a young person in your community and in your own family. Master the financial game with a fresh, ground-

---

24 Amos Joel created a switching device in 1972 that opened doors for the cell phone industry. Available at www.nytimes.com/2008/10/28/technology/28joel.html
25 Inventor of the Week Archive. Laserphaco Probe. [updated Feb. 2005; cited 2008]. <http://web.mit.edu/invent/iow/bath.html>

ed mind. Allow trans-generational wealth to begin or continue with you. The way to steadily make improvements is to empower those that can continue the legacy and benefit humanity.

West African Symbol for readiness, steadfastness and hardiness

Chapter Five
The Making of a Zeallionaire

There are many wonderful possibilities emerging from our nation's expanding global consciousness. One is the awakened, spiritually-grounded millionaire. The creative genius of this type of millionaire brings fresh ideas to individuals, businesses and communities. This millionaire has a zeal for bringing out the goodness in humanity. Zeal is "the fervor or tireless devotion for a person, cause, or ideal and determination in its furtherance." [26] The Zeallionaire is a spiritually grounded millionaire with zeal. The expression of her or his "fervor and tireless devotion" is demonstrated in her or his line of business or philanthropic activity. Former U.S. Vice President Al Gore is a prime example of a Zeallionaire making a global impact. Gore has created an awareness of global warming through the documentary *An Inconvenient Truth*. The former Vice President used his prominence to share strategies to reduce the effects of global warming worldwide. Zeallionaires expand their reach by having a "good perception of history [in order to] have a better understanding of the past and present, and thus a clear vision of the future."[27]

---

26 Available at <www.Wiktionary.com>
27 Quote from Carlos Slim Helu, one of the top three wealthiest people on the Western Hemisphere 1994; Available at <http://video.forbes.com/fvn/billion-

Zeallionaires don't sit around waiting for opportunity to knock on their doors. They don't expect an instant windfall of a million bucks to be handed to them. No. Zeallionaires take their acquired knowledge and they knock on the door of opportunity. We all have heard the saying "knowledge is power".[28] This power is intangible and therefore can never be taken away. It is the kind of knowledge that must be actively sought. Zeallionaires realize that if all their worldly possessions were to somehow disappear, their knowledge and resourcefulness would allow them to reacquire those material possessions. In this sense, Zeallionaires also demonstrate a level of fearlessness. Aspiring Zeallionaires must exhibit the same kind of fearlessness. When we allow ourselves to break through fear and apprehension, we can readily advance in our careers, businesses and our lives. Let knowledge, embraced by the will of our Creator, be the battering ram that knocks down the door of fear and apprehension so that we may enter into our new lives.

The forefathers of this nation broke down many doors as they entered new lives of previously unchartered freedoms. In order to separate themselves from oppressive rule they reverted back to the "assum[ed] powers of the earth." Our forefathers recognized these powers to be "the separate and equal station to which the Laws of Nature and of Nature's God entitled them." The Declaration of Independence further describes "these truths to be self-evident, that all men are created equal, that they are endowed by their Creator with certain inalienable rights that among these are life, liberty and the pursuit of happiness. That to secure these rights, governments are instituted among men, deriving their just

---

aires-2010/top-billionaire-slim-gates-buffett>.
28 Dan Harmon. School House Rock. *Knowledge is Power.* 1973 ©

powers from the consent of the governed."[29] The founders of this nation clearly understood these basic human rights even though they did not agree that truly *all* humans should enjoy them. Knowledge of our fundamental human rights can have a profound effect on our lives, especially in the pursuit of peace, harmony and abundance. The "pursuit of happiness" is our basic right and is the fundamental component to becoming a Zeallionaire. It aligns with our freedom to pursue our passions, enhance our skills and talents and to be a benefit to humanity. This basic right puts us on the road to wealth, meaning the condition of well being.

The impact of knowing our personal history can be as profound as knowing our nation's history. "In every conceivable manner, the family is the link to our past and a bridge to our future." [30] Knowing who we are can be a motivating factor for getting us on the road to wealth.

Far too many of us walk around disconnected from our culture, unaware of our purpose in life and subsequently have no idea of who we really are nor what we are capable of becoming. In a documentary produced by PBS entitled *African American Lives 2*, Chris Rock stated he stumbled into becoming a comedian. Upon discovering his great-great grandfather served in the Civil War after being a slave for 21 years, Rock said he would have had a direction for his future as a youth "because it would have taken away the [thought] that he was going to be nothing." The value of knowing our past, whether positive or negative, can have a profound effect on the types of wealth we choose to experience over our lives.

Christopher Gardner was particularly moved by words in the Declaration of Independence. Mr. Gardner did not know

---

29 Jefferson, Thomas. *The Declaration of Independence*. 1776. Available at <http://www.ushistory.org/declaration/document/>
30 Haley, Alex quotation.

his father until he was 28 years old. Because of this, Gardner vowed to be a good father and to not follow in his father's foot steps. This very powerful affirmation defines Mr. Gardner's character. The integrity born from that affirmation is evident in how Gardner cared for his son during a rough period in his life. Despite experiences with life-altering challenges, Gardner took the steps that lead him from poverty to wealth. Again it is important we know our personal histories. We can start by consulting our elders about their lives, the lessons they learned and what they want to pass on to us. The steps can open the door to our development into Zeallionaire.

As we travel up the road to becoming Zeallionaires we must arm ourselves with the knowledge needed to become financially independent. It is important that we surround ourselves with trusted individuals who specialize in finance. It should be clear that the United States was founded on two basic principals: religious and economic freedom. People fled Europe to the "New World" for the opportunity to pursue happiness regardless of social ranking. This new awakening of our nation allows the basic principles of freedom to exist now, for all, more than ever. To be fully prepared, knowledge of our financial system must be acquired to strategically attain and maintain wealth.

The most efficient way to create, build and maintain wealth is via strategic tax strategies. When we look at the tax system we see that there are many benefits for individuals that own property, investments and businesses. It is not so beneficial for individuals with only an earned income. A key to creating wealth is to have more than just earned income from W-2 wages. Sustainable wealth is created when we invest in resources that generate unearned income from assets. Assets can be redefined as money you can put in your pocket today or at some point in the future to ultimately enhance and improve your lifestyle. When investing or starting a business, it is best to consider the tax implications before, during and after we invest. People who closely consider the tax implication prior to taking on major investments have better chances of maximizing profits and income.

Although taxes are inevitable, it is interesting to note that there was a time in the early part of our history when Americans were not accessed a tax on their personal income tax. The Civil War initiated the first levy of income tax on American citizens in 1861, generating $375 million of revenue. When the war ended the income tax was repealed. Everything went back to normal. People had full access to their hard-earned money and the government financed its operations primarily from customs duties (tariffs).[31] Over thirty years later, the government needed to raise additional monies for the War Revenue Act of 1899 and accessed federal income tax on individuals to fund the Spanish-American war. The opponents of this tax successfully challenged its constitutionality. However, in 1909, Congress was able to pass a law to tax the income from real and personal property because it was treated as an excise tax. From 1873 to 1907, the U.S. experienced a great deal of economic issues increasing the need for a centralized bank. In 1893, a banking panic sparked the worst depression the U.S. had ever experienced. Had it not been for the financial mogul J.P. Morgan, the crisis would have lasted much longer. The solution to creating stability was to create a centralized banking system. President Woodrow Wilson signed the Sixteenth Amendment of the U.S. Constitution in 1913. A central-

---

31 Willis/Hoffman/Maloney/Raabe. *South-Western Federal Taxation Comprehensive: Volume 2010 edition*. Chapter 1 page 1-3, 1-2 History of U.S. Taxation. 2010.

ized bank was established and a federal tax on earned income was accessed. [32,33]

Knowing the history of the U.S. tax system is empowering. It gives us insight as to why things are the way they are. To put it simply, Congress made it law. Congress also created the Internal Revenue Service (IRS). This regulatory body is filled with rules that access a tax and rules that allow a reduction or exemption from being taxed. The key is to know what assets have the most favorable tax benefits. Property owners, business owners and investors receive the greatest tax benefits. So, in order to take full advantage of capitalism, monetize God-given gifts through a business and/or property ownership. Hire a CPA to legally, strategically and efficiently work the tax system. People have been creating sustainable wealth for years. The knowledge they gained by knowing the specific tax laws to maintain their wealth is priceless.

Clearly, we see that knowledge from a broad perspective in terms of our history and a more focused view in terms of tax incentives creates a power that cannot be taken away. It also evokes a sense of confidence that results in the security that regardless of current circumstances, sustainable wealth can always be acquired.

---

32 The History of the Federal Reserve <www.federalreserveeducation.org/about-the-fed/history/>
33 *History of the Tax System.* [cited 2009]. <http://www.treas.gov/education/fact-sheets/taxes/ustax.shtml>

West African symbol of support, cooperation and encouragement

Chapter Six
The Development of Generational Zeallionaires

Playwright and novelist Thornton Wilder said, "Money is like manure; it's not worth a thing unless it is spread around encouraging young things to grow." It is imperative that we not only educate ourselves on financial matters, we must educate our young people as well. This education should begin in the home and be supported in our schools. Once these seeds are planted, they should be reinforced by encouraging our children to gain exposure and experience in business along with investing and exploring career options. Talking to our children about money management and investing will invariably lead to better financial outcomes for them. If a child begins working in high school or, better yet, starts a business and, over a four-year period, saves $100 per month ($3.33 per day) at a 5% interest rate, he or she would accumulate about $5,300. If the child continued this practice through college, he or she would save about $12,000. Consider this in relation to the typical situation of having graduated with no money saved and a mountain of debt. What a way to launch a career. It behooves us, then, to start early to teach our children about the money and how to make better money decisions. Studies have shown people who learned about financial matters at a young age do better in reaching financial goals.[34] Learning about healthy money matters at home first and then reinforced in school is integral to the development of Zeallionaires. This knowledge must be passed on and enhanced for generations. Albeit optimistic, financial literacy in our educational system is vital to beginning the process to reverse the dummying down of America, especially as it relates to financial literacy. There is more to life than money. However, money is the means to which life experiences are enhanced. A lack of financial literacy programs in our school systems correlates to a lack of preparedness many baby boomers are facing as they enter retirement. In addition, the vast solicitations encouraging consumerism versus saving is a great credit to insufficient resources at retirement. The challenge is that our educational system is in constant development with finding solutions to our ever-changing society. However, when it comes to fundamentals, the mindset and behaviors that create wealth are everlasting. The three stages and seven elements expressed in this book are timeless. As the food revolution enters schools, financial literacy should follow. A healthier, financially savvy American can lead to a brighter future for the world.

    We can all do our parts. Parents and teachers can do their parts at home. They can also insist that financial literacy be a requirement in the curriculum. Attend PTA and community council meetings and set an intention to have a financial literacy class in your school's curriculum. Junior Achievement, a nationwide non-profit organization, has classroom ready programs that educate young people on money matters. Community leaders, financial professionals, superinten-

---

34 Available at <http://www.chicagofed.org/>

dents, principals and state officials have spent years discussing the importance of incorporating financial literacy. Only three states have made it mandatory in their curriculum: Utah, Missouri and Tennessee. There are only eighteen states that require personal finance to be incorporated into other subject matter; AZ, CO, GA, ID, IL, IN, KA, LA, NC, NH, NY, OH, OK, SC, SD, TX, VA, and WV. Thirty-two states dismiss financial literacy altogether.[35] The reason why there has been years of discussion on the matter is that student curriculum is already packed and there is a lack of understanding as to determine how to categorize financial literacy. If it is to be incorporated, under what discipline should it be categorized; social studies, mathematics, economics or its own subject? Incorporating financial literacy into school curriculums has been an issue since the 1970s, but only since 2006 has it become a major topic of consideration. It is past time for action. End the debate and classify it as a separate topic since money affords us access to the tangible things we need in our current society: food, clothing, transportation, shelter, medical care and other necessities and luxuries in life. Incorporating financial literacy programs as a mandatory curriculum in the school system offers a great solution to create a more financially savvy nation and the creation of generational Zeallionaires. However, as with most important lessons, it begins at home. Generational wealth happens when families make legacy planning an integral component of their family life. Zeallionaires create legacies that leave our children and our world better off than the one we inherited.

What exactly is legacy planning or transgenerational wealth? It is the process of transferring wealth during our

---

35 Available at <http://www.jumpstart.org/state-financial-education-requirements.html>

lifetime and upon death to our loved ones. Some may know or understand this better as: estate planning. Determining who or what organization will receive our remaining assets is the ultimate stage in the wealth-building process. This is how wealth is circulated and channeled to people and organizations that matter to us most. It is integral that legacy planning is incorporated at each stage of our life planning to have better control over our money. If you don't plan, don't worry; the government will plan for you. It's called probate. This is the legal process that determines how our hard-earned money will be distributed if we do not make the provisions ourselves. Proper legacy planning can range from simple to complex strategies. A simple way to plan is to name a beneficiary on all of our investments and bank accounts. More complex planning involves the establishment of a trust, of which there are many types and strategies. A trust is a document that allows an individual, the creator (or grantor), to determine who will receive our remaining wealth, how much they will receive, when they will receive it, and who shall serve as trustee to make sure our directions are executed. A common concern raised in legacy planning is the financial responsibility of the non-profit organization or the heirs.

Financial literacy along with a solid work ethic are factors that should be taught early on. Unfortunately, many of us who have created wealth achieved this on our own and did not teach this to our children. There are estate planning strategies that can address this very issue. Many people create foundations to give some or all of their money to a charity or they create a trust that has terms and agreements the heir must adhere to in order to receive the money. The ultimate goal is to create enough money to address our current and future needs over our entire lifetime where our money is working for us regardless of market conditions. This is sustainable wealth. When we plan for abundance we end up with a legacy that can be passed on to the next generation. This excess money would normally go to the government if no provisions are made. By planning for abundance we are in control of our money in the present and beyond. We are able to determine how our hard-earned dollars are to be used if we become mentally or physically unstable. Additionally, we are able to control who or what organization benefits from our legacy. This is how wealth is circulated. It is critical that we support our youth by exposing them to financial literacy as early as possible. This starts with an understanding that creating and securing a solid financial future reverts back to the three stages of creating sustainable wealth: knowledge, planning and tenacity. We must take it upon ourselves to continue to learn and educate others on financial matters.

West African Symbol for Good Fortune and Sanity

Chapter Seven
Becoming a Zeallionaire

The path to becoming a Zeallionaire is predicated on the levels of wealth we experience on a day-to-day basis. Zeallionaires are wealthy first because they are able to experience joy from the inside out. The relationships they maintain are based on how they bring added value to others, which, in turn, enhances their own well being. Monetary wealth merely provides additional options and enhances the wealth that already exists. It is critical to be clear of this distinction. People often equate and often confuse having a lot of money with joy, success and happiness, or simply having it all. There are many people who are successful monetarily and still have shallow relationships, suffer from depression, experience constant family drama or are plagued with physical illness. Money in and of itself is not what makes a Zeallionaire; it is what we do with money that makes a Zeallionaire.

In the book *Simple Wisdom for Living Rich,* Oseola McCarthy, a philanthropist during the late 1800s, shares her views of success. For more than 70 years, McCarthy lived a simple life taking care of her needs without being wasteful. McCarthy made a living washing clothes, and was a diligent saver. At the age of 88 she donated $150,000 to the University of Southern Mississippi to help disadvantaged students. Mrs. McCarthy donated this large portion of her savings as a living gift versus a provision in her will upon death. There are others just like her. Eartha M. M. White, born in 1876, accumulated over one million dollars throughout her life time. White donated almost all of her profits from her private investments and entrepreneurial ventures to finance multiple humanitarian causes; Biddy Mason, a savvy real estate investor in the late 1800s became the wealthiest black women in California. Mason gave to charities and was the founder of First AME Church, the first black Church in Los Angeles; Jacob Lawrence, an artist and painter known for illustrating the history and struggles of African Americans, founded The Gwendolyn Knight and Jacob Lawrence Fellowship. Through this fellowship black artists are eligible to receive $10,000 to further their artistic practice. Many, if not most, of the previously mentioned philanthropist did not have the abundant opportunities and resources we all have today. Moreover, you will notice that the examples cited here date back to the 19th century. What about more recent examples? Of course, there are people to cite who implement sound cash flow management today, but they are few and far between. Prior to the creation of installment notes in the late 1800s as explained in chapter three, people actually saved money before they made purchases. After the Great Depression hit in 1929, the people most affected by the depression stopped saving; however, they did not use credit either. It is this generation we must look to as a model for conscious spending. They lived within their means not on credit and survived on ingenuity while efficiently using resources. Today we live in a throwaway society where we are constantly bombarded with advertisements that encourage excess spending and borrowing. We live in a disposable society where we are more likely to trash something that could have been recycled, reused or repurposed. Today, the national savings rate is about 6%[36], up from the near 0% in the beginning of the 21st century. It is still well below the 9% people saved in the 1980s.[37] Cash is king. It is critical that we shift our habits to that of conscious spending. Save 15% to 20% of your gross income while giving at least 10% to charity is an ideal strategy. It takes planning and it is doable, even in high-cost-of-living states like, California, Florida and Hawaii. Zeallionaires have the capacity to shift gears and allow themselves to benefit from the multiple opportunities and resources available to them.

In a world where we are able to get access to information at the click of a button, we can get information overload and end up taking no action or the wrong action. We are bombarded with a variety of books, seminars, television shows, webinars and podcasts on what we should do with our money. Yet many of us live our lives financially disorganized; we are teeming with uncertainty about the future. Some of us are planning for scarcity and just don't know it yet. This disorganization exists because the fundamentals are not apart of our daily routines. Clarity and certainty can be realized by practicing the fundamentals, which is the plan for abundance. Interestingly enough there are very few resources that enlighten us on the

---

36 http://www.washingtonpost.com/wp-dyn/content/article/2010/08/03/AR2010080305317.html
37 Guidolin and La Jeunesse. *The Decline in the US Personal Savings Rate: Is It real and Is It a Puzzle?* Available at http://docs.google.com/viewer?a=v&q=cache:DLMfE8mLymwJ:research.stlouisfed.org/publications/review/07/11/Guidolin.pdf+personal+saving+rate+in+us&hl=en&gl=us&pid=bl&-srcid=ADGEESgku4u7W3QLDiK-yMrLmJhGFbM3ovb4nsOWOy6ZSPnZcmiPOgPrdG4w lYKDUxLIA3PCrothZgxvqb2gtVt9Zr0u3dNqsLYpiu1AipMb8zW6JKJsAbyqx EyIGjprkX8DWYltA8jX&sig=AHIEtbS8Zb20dccZHhXhUL4S5AjobHPNRA

essentials in a way that aligns the various aspects of our financial life to create the proper financial balance that directs us on a path of sustainability while addressing the other aspects of wealth that is not money. Henry David Thoreau said it best, "wealth is the ability to fully experience life."

The significance of the fundamentals is preeminent in the life of John Wooden, the late basketball coach for UCLA. It is well known that he focused on the basics. For example, in every practice he coached players on how to tie their shoes. Think about that. Imagine there are three seconds left in the game and a star player is going for the tie breaker and trips over his shoelaces. People do this with their finances all the time. They build a financial house by first putting in the landscape, the pool, and crown molding. All of these features are fun and pretty to look at but they don't ensure that our house is built on a solid foundation. As soon as a storm hits, the lack of proper insulation and protection brings immediate damage to our wealth. There is a tendency to address the aesthetic matters in our life instead of protecting wealth efficiently as it accumulates over time. A vast majority of Americans begin to build wealth by investing in high-risk investments or acquire debt via a mortgage before they have done the groundwork to protect their current wealth from unnecessary loss.

The plan for abundance starts with the fundamentals and via protection of all the wealth we have acquired to this point. It creates financial order and provides clarity on whether we are on the path to sustainable wealth or not. Note again that sustainable wealth is the amount of money necessary to take care of both our current and future incomes over our entire lives. The objective is to have our money working for us versus always having to work for our money. The key is to position our money in a way that will allow us to have all of our financial concerns met and not be affected by the ebbs and flows of the stock, bond or real estate markets.

How does your financial house look?

Plan of Scarcity   Plan of Abundance

We explored the foundation of attaining sustainable wealth by being knowledgeable in key areas quite extensively. The empowerment received from this knowledge allows us to move into the practical planning phase of attaining sustainable wealth. If we are not in the proper mental, emotional and physical environment, knowledge alone will not lead to wealth. It would be challenging to enjoy the pleasures monetary wealth brings if we are too stressed, holding on to the pains of parental neglect or connected to life support in a hospital. The planning phase has to be approached with a foundation of mental, emotional and physical well being. Having a healthy mind, evoking positive emotions and maintaining good physical health is a part of creating, building and maintaining sustainable wealth. This is the lifestyle of a Zeallionaire.

African Symbol for Independence, Freedom, Emancipation

Chapter Eight
Plan for Abundance

The Plan for Abundance is the financial road map for living life on purpose. It is designed to protect the assets you currently own, increase your income, help ensure a solid financial future and create a legacy that benefits humanity for generations. This can be accomplished with a plan orchestrated by a team of financial professionals where you are the conductor. The plan for abundance is centered on what matters to you most; it is discovered when you ask yourself what is important to you about money? You must ask yourself this question more than once to really get to the core of your values as they relate to the Five Aspects of the Human Experience.

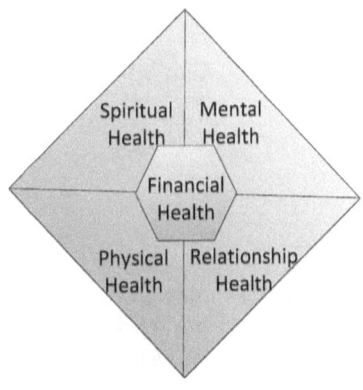

Five Aspects of the Human Experience

If you want to progress, you must plan. As the saying goes, "most people do not plan to fail, but fail to plan." The plan for abundance puts you on the right track to sustainable wealth. There are seven elements to creating sustainable wealth. Many of these elements are accomplished simultaneously while others must be completed before anything else. In the same way you are unique, the plan for abundance also has a distinct plan design. The following provides the basic concepts of each element; it affords you the opportunity to insert your unique goals and ideas that lead to sustainable wealth. Before the planning phase you should ascertain where you are now and where you want to go? Categorize a list of your current assets and liabilities using a balance sheet[38] followed by a list of your goals. A sample balance sheet is included in the back of this book. Your goals need to be SMART—Specific, Measurable, Actionable, Realistic and Time oriented. Your goals should be divided into immediate (next 30-90 days), short term (90 days - 12 mo), mid term (1-10) and long term (10+) years. If there is trouble, take a moment and be still. Think about your life's purpose. Why are you here? Visualize what and how you want your life to be in various phases. Create a life purpose and/or mission statement.

---

[38] Assets are tangible and intangible things you own that have monetary value. Liabilities are personal and business debts. When you categorize your assets and liabilities you are creating a balance sheet, which ultimately determines your net worth. Asset minus Liabilities = Net Worth

> ## Life Purpose Statement
>
> _____
> _____
> _____
>
> **SMART Goals:**
> •Immediate (30 – 90 days)
>
>
> •Short Term (90 day – 12 months)
>
>
> •Medium Term (1-10 yrs)
>
>
> •Long Term (10+ yrs)

Remember to start from where you are now. Being comfortable with your current financial situation, whether it's starting a career, debt overload, rebuilding wealth after a market crash or making sure your legacy is passed on in the manner you see fit, is essential. Knowing where you are and where you want to go is the foundation for maneuvering strategically throughout the elements of the plan for abundance.

The plan for abundance is rigorous. We know, however, that anything worth having is worth working for because it is highly rewarding. To stay on track and accomplish the goal requires motivation. The exercise below will help you to dig deeper at finding your purpose and establishing your goals. To determine motivational factors, begin asking the following questions and then ask why?

- What do I want in the next 90 days? What about 5, 10 or 20 years from now? Why?

- When do I want to retire or be financially independent where my money is working for me versus me working for my money? Why?

- At a certain point in the future, what would be impossible to live without? (food, shelter, transportation, travel, visiting grandchildren, sailing, playing golf, volunteering, etcetera.) Why?

- If basic needs are met, then what would I need to make my life really comfortable and enjoyable? (Hire a private chef, travel or visit your vacation home quarterly versus annually.) Why?

- Assuming basic needs are met and I am comfortable and enjoying life, what would life be like if I could do what I wanted when I wanted? (spend time promoting a great cause, igniting social change for the benefit of humanity, becoming a venture capitalist to young entrepreneurs, traveling in a private jet, or reinventing yourself) Why?

Whatever this future may be, write it down and consider the following categories:

> *Survival Lifestyle* – one who has just enough to pay monthly expenses.

> *Comfortable Lifestyle* – one who has enough to pay bills and enjoy life with only a few compro-

mises. In other words, there may be a need to save up or wait to go on trips, add amenities to the house or limit entertainment expenses.

Sustainable Lifestyle – one who is able to do whatever, whenever and can give monetarily as much and as often as opportunities become present.

LIFE STYLE PYRAMID

There is no right or wrong. The categories are meant to alert you to the path you are currently on. As you review your current financial situation determine where you are currently headed; survival, comfortable or sustainable. If you find that you are on track to survival and you desire a sustainable lifestyle, let that reality be an encouraging factor to shift your mindset to a Zeallionaire.

Element One: Cash Flow

One key to creating sustainable wealth is being fully aware of your inflows and outflows. Cash flow is king! If your annual income is $25,000 or $25,000,000, spending more than what you take home will be a financial TKO (technical knock out). You will have to shift your behavior to that of a Zeallionaire and monitor your spending. Use of a cash flow statement (see appendix) is important when evaluating where your money is coming from and where it is going. Keep receipts and account for your expenditures daily, weekly or monthly. It is best to account for your spending at least weekly because you want to be as accurate as possible. Many things happen over the course of a month and it is easy to overlook expenditures, especially if they are small. If you find that your current spending habits are not aligned with your goals, then you must shift and change those habits. Remember, habits can be developed in 52 days. An excellent habit to establish that will work for any income is the 50/30/20 rule. 50% of your after tax income goes to necessities, 30% to wants and 20% to savings. It is pivotal to note that how you spend your money is crucial to wealth building. This can not be expressed enough. If you don't monitor your spending and live within your means, you critically hinder your path toward sustainable wealth. Countless millionaires have mismanaged their money resulting in bankruptcy. Mark Twain, author of *Tom Sawyer* and other popular novels, filed for bankruptcy in 1894. MC Hammer, a popular hip hop artist in the 90s, filed bankruptcy because he tried to help too many friends and family, which put him at risk. Ulysses S. Grant, our 18th President, filed bankruptcy in 1884. J. Fife Symington, Governor of Arizona, filed in 1995 while still in office. James Wilson, U.S. Supreme court justice, filed bankruptcy in 1798. Larry King, late night talk show host, filed in 1978.[39] Of course, there are more people that were once materially wealthy and at some point in their careers ended up filing bankruptcy. Anyone can get off track.

---

39 Information available at <www.grandlawfirm.com>

The U. S. financial system is designed to help you get back on track, albeit with some consequences. It is better not to venture down this road. Develop the habit of monitoring expenses. Review the summaries of your monthly spending at a minimum and adjust accordingly.

Element Two: Asset Protection Strategies

Properly protecting assets is one of the first things you should do when creating, building and maintaining sustainable wealth. Insurance and other protection strategies have their place, and there is an order of priority. The most important asset to protect is the one that tends to get protected the least, you. *You* are your greatest asset. Protect yourself and your abilities first. In other words, purchase health and disability insurance. Maintaining good health affords you the opportunity to generate a desired income and lifestyle. Should any major health issues arise, health insurance, albeit expensive, should help pay for your needed care without depleting your cash reserves. The idea behind the current health reform is to create better opportunities for all Americans to receive better and more affordable care, which will in turn put less pressure on personal savings for medical expenses.

Income protection, also known as disability insurance, is one of the most overlooked forms of protection. It is an integral foundational block in creating sustainable wealth. If your ability to produce an income is hindered or ceases, your financial house can crumble. When some people think of disability insurance they typically think of a person in a wheelchair. A solid disability plan covers much more than being bound to a wheelchair. Most disabilities are temporary and last less than five years. [40] A quality income protection plan will allow you to receive a portion of your income if or when you are unable to perform work duties.

---

40 Bureau of Labor Statistics <www.bls.gov>

Be mindful that every policy will have its own definition of disability. There are different provisions to take note of when comparing coverage. Ideally you want a policy that has a true own occupation clause because it provides the most optimal protection of your income. Other clauses like modified own occupation and any occupation provide income protection however it is limited. The own occupation clause states that if you were totally disabled in your regular occupation you would receive your full disability monthly benefit even if you chose to work in another gainful occupation after suffering the total disability. There are different provisions to take note of when comparing coverage, especially when you analyze group benefits verses an individual policy. Take a moment to read up on the options and work with a competent financial professional to help you find the company and policy that meets your needs. The essential point to note here is that you have to really understand the importance of the coverage. If you can generate an income from and income producing asset, like cash flow from real estate then you can consider this as possible income in the event of a disability. However, this kind of income is not guaranteed and has to be physically managed. When it comes to disability we tend to think we are invincible. However, take a moment to remember the last time you had a cold or flu. No, really, stop and think about it. You did not feel like doing much of anything, right? Now imagine feeling like that for six to 18 months. Based on your current financial situation, would you be able to sustain your lifestyle with ease? How about dealing with a tenant? Not having an appropriate amount of disability insurance in place may cause unnecessary financial ruin or force some people to deplete their personal wealth. Review your current disability insurance policies and make sure they are on par with current incomes or establish new policies.

Car insurance is mandated by the state and many, if not most, drivers have coverage. However, more often than not, the liability coverage is not coordinated with homeowner's insurance. In a highly litigious society, protecting yourself from being sued is another way to protect your wealth. Make sure your liability limits on your car insurance and homeowner's coverage are at least equal to your net worth, and at best, maxed out. For those that have or need more liability coverage, incorporating an umbrella policy can fill the gap. The purpose of an umbrella policy is to cover the personal liability gap of your car and homeowner's insurance. The value of the umbrella policy should be at least equal or greater than your net worth. If you have a net worth in excess of $500,000, you want to consider the benefits of umbrella policies. The policies generally start at $1 million and increase from there. Here is an example of how an umbrella policy works: Say you were to get into an accident or someone slipped and fell on your property and sued for $1.2 million. You have acquired $500,000 in your retirement plan,[41] $50,000 in a 529 College Savings Plan, $650,000 in home equity and $75,000 in mutual funds and savings, totaling $1,275,000, assuming no debt. The liability coverage on your homeowner's and car insurance equal $200,000. Where do you think the plaintiff's attorney is going to go for the other $1.1 million? Your personal assets. This leaves you with $75,000 in funds. When an attorney is determining how much to sue for, they use a formula called the human life value. This is the monetary amount a person is worth based on their age, current income and the future potential income that person could have made over their life expectancy. If there was an umbrella policy in place of at least $2 million, then none of your assets would be marked to cover that person's potential life time income. Incor-

---

[41] Note that some retirement plans have creditor protection up to certain limits based on the state legislation.

porating a cost efficient umbrella policy allows your financial life and lifestyle to continue seamlessly. Keep in mind that if you create a layered savings plan as suggested in the third element, you benefit greatly from higher deductibles. Increasing deductibles in addition to liability limits keeps cost levels down and, in some cases, lowers premium costs. Call your insurance agent today to shelter your wealth from unknown threats.

Life insurance is a more commonly talked about form of protection than income protection insurance. There are many theories about whether term or permanent life insurance is better. To end the confusion, the policy that pays surviving heirs the death benefit income tax free at the time of demise and provides for the heirs in the best possible way is the best policy to own. There are major differences with term and permanent life insurance. Term insurance can be compared to renting. It covers the need at a low cost and does not build any *equity*. You own term insurance for a set number of years, typically 20 years or in increments of 5, 10 or 30 years. You can also purchase annual renewable term insurance. Permanent insurance, however, provides you with more options. It is like owning a house. You typically pay more up front and are able to build up *equity* in the form of cash value. Owning permanent insurance affords you the opportunity to receive very favorable tax benefits, distinctly different from any other type of tax favorable investment. The cash value of a policy usually grows taxed deferred. As the owner of the policy you can access the available cash value at any time for any reason. This is very different from tax deferred accounts like IRA's, 403B's, 401K's, and 457's. The government and possibly your employer has placed limitations on when and how you can access the account value. Some people borrow or withdraw from the policy value of the life insurance to pay for college, make a down payment for property or supplement retirement income. Using high cash value life insurance as an asset is a viable way to build sustainable wealth. Be mindful that any time a distribution is made from the policy values of a permanent policy the death benefit will decrease, it could negatively impact overall policy values and may be subject to taxes. Always engage in council before you make a distribution. It is critical to note that first and for most life insurance is primarily for the financial well being of heirs. There are other reasons to own life insurance including: creating a legacy, paying estate taxes, extra income for retirement, capital for business ventures, protecting a partner's business interest and, the main reason, to provide for the financial well-being of surviving heirs. The question to address now is the amount. Most advisors and clients use a needs approach, which answers the question of how much will one need for a particular purpose? The needs analysis considers the cost of the funeral, education costs, emergency expenses, mortgages, and retirement for the surviving spouse. The major flaw in the needs approach is that it does not consider the loss of income potential based on the talents and contributions of the deceased. It is in alignment with the plan for survival. Loved ones that pass prematurely never get the opportunity to create, build or expand on their ideas or business ventures. These projects could have enhanced their family's life experiences as well as the value it could have brought to humanity. The value a person brings to family, friends and the community is impossible to determine.

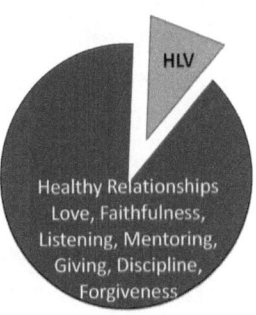

In the world of finance, a very small slice of your total worth can be calculated. The economist, Solomon Huebner,[42] called this the Human Life Value. As described earlier in this chapter, it is the financial slice of the person's value. It is based on the potential income you could make over a life time based on current income. Again, this is the same formula that lawyers use to determine value in the case of a lawsuit. For those that are of an entrepreneurial mindset this can be very limiting because, who is to say what is the greatest amount of income one can produce? Nevertheless, using the Human Life Value formula will allow for more coverage than the Needs Approach to protect and maintain the financial well-being of surviving heirs. Our creator placed us here to live a life of abundance, not scarcity. An abundance life is where all concerns are met with grace and ease, versus a life of scarcity, where lack and limitations exist. We do not have to force the next generation to recreate the wheel. Follow the plan for abundance to create a life of multiple opportunities now. Fortune 500 companies buy permanent life insurance for key executives that provide substantial wealth building benefits to both the company and the executive. This is an efficient use of permanent life insurance while we are living. Why not use it to provide more options to ensure sustainable wealth now and for generations to come?

Long term care is a great concern for the baby boomer generation. Due to advanced medicine and healthy living life spans have increased. The need for care as we age has increased as well. Studies show that of the couples turning 65, 70% will need some form of long term care services. The average annual cost of care nationwide is $64,000[43]. Despite this reality people have not considered the financial impact and family dynamics caused by long term care. Without proper funding for possible expenses

---

[42] http://www.bankinsurance.com/editorial/articles/pdfs/bim/1993-philosophy-of-life-insurance.pdf
[43] Information available at <www.guidetolongtermcare.com>

incurred for long term care, savings can be wiped out and lifestyle greatly reduced. If Medicare[44] is a part of your plan, be aware that Medicare only covers skilled nursing care not long term care. The various limitations under the Medicare program are in alignment with the plan for scarcity. It may suffice as a back up if all else fails but it is not the plan Zeallionaires rely on. Proper coverage is a secure way to supplement or fully fund for long term care.

Concern regarding long term care is not an individual decision although it may seem that way. Care usually becomes the responsibility of the children and more often the daughter(s) more so than son(s). When there are resources to address the parent's long term care expenses, the children are at least relieved from having to pay out of their own pockets. This makes it easier to endure the process as mom, dad or other relatives' age. In some instances parents are not in the position financially to afford a long term care policy and state options are not satisfactory. In these circumstances it would behoove the children to consider purchasing a long term care policy on their parents. It is probable that the need for care of parents will come when you are at the height of your career, married and/or with children.

The benefits of the long term care policy extend beyond the financial benefits. It allows those in the sandwich generation to supervise the care versus providing the care. A long term care policy provides additional options to the care givers instead of having to take off work or retiring earlier than planned. Schedule a family meeting to discuss the advantages of long term care for your loved ones.

There are other specialty coverages that are designed for certain niches like business overhead expense and watercraft policies. They provide policy owners with specific peril protection. Although the coverage is narrow in scope, it is a prudent strategy

---

[44] For California residence the public program is Medical.

to shelter ourselves from an unexpected potential catastrophic loss. Remember, the amount it costs to protect your financial well-being is far less than the price you may pay if you have to start from scratch.

Zeallionaires are good financial stewards with the assets they acquire from the income they generated based on the use of their God-given skills, talents and resources. The assets are first and foremost protected. Take this time to behave like a Zeallionaire. Review, renew and establish relevant protection strategies.

Element Three: Savings and Debt Reduction

Having a savings plan is necessary to create and maintain sustainable wealth. It is critical in that it is your safety net. Saving directly from ones income was a common practice that resulted in significant wealth for many Americans in the early to mid 1900s. A shift from saving to credit card spending and relying on investment return to create a nest egg is in part what encouraged many people to save less. Over time, Americans became increasingly indebted to bankers in the form of credit card debt, mortgages and short term financing. A debt obligation to bankers was one of the fears some of our forefathers, congressmen, presidents and citizens harbored as far back as 1791.[45]

Debt, when properly managed, can create wealth building opportunities. When debt is mismanaged it is a drag on wealth-building opportunities. The need to address saving and debt reduction concurrently is essential. Strategically dumping debt increases current and future opportunities to save more. Debt is the main reason why Americans are not saving like the traditional generation, those born between 1922 and 1945. This generation saved money before making major or minor purchases. Following generations developed the urgency to buy and have things

---

45 The History Box <http://thehistorybox.com>

now instead of waiting, creating a society of over consumption. To become better managers of debt, first, you must shift your thinking about debt. This will result in changing your habit of acquiring debt. Next, begin a dumping debt program by using the factoring method enclosed in the appendix. Make a personal commitment to dump the debt. Declare it to a person you trust to help hold you accountable. There is a great tendency to dump debt and not save. This is strongly discouraged. The reason credit card debt is acquired often times is because there was no savings. You must save as you dump the debt. The idea is that as your debt decreases your savings capacity increases. This is the see-saw effect. This new habit can provide you with financial well-being now and well into the future.

A solid savings plan should be broken into two parts. One part addresses immediate, short and medium-term needs while the second part addresses long-term needs. Depending on your goals and the time horizon, you should save anywhere between 10% and 25% of your net income, at least, and at best your gross income. As this is generally a challenge for most, it is wise to begin in stages. The key is to be consistent. In the classic children's story of the Tortoise and the Hare, the tortoise won the race because it was focused on the end result.

Part one of the savings plans has three stages. The first stage is to create a *dip account*™ to build up enough funds to cover at least one month of your expenses. Only allow yourself to dip into this account when something out of the norm occurs. For example, if you were invited to a celebration on short notice, one that required special attire. Perhaps there is a need to fly home to take care of a family member or you need to repair your car. Use this account for such events. The caveat is that you are only to use up to a certain amount. Say your monthly personal expenses are $3,000 per month. Then $3,000 is the amount you should have saved in the dip account. You must put a stop limit on how much you can spend before you get into dangerous territory, perhaps 50%. However much you decide, commit to it and stay steadfast. If or when you tap into this immediate savings, the next month needs to be devoted to replenishing the dip account.

Stage two requires that you set aside three to 12 months of the total amount of your monthly expenses or gross income in an *emergency fund*.[46] If you were to become sick or get laid off, this account will allow three to 12 months of relief until something else kicks in such as disability income insurance, a new job or funding from a business venture.

The final stage of the savings plan expands your wealth and horizons; it requires a *wealth account*. This account is solely for the purpose of building capital to buy income-generating or appreciating assets. Your dip, emergency, and wealth account must be separate for transparency. Disciplined saving means keeping your dip account and your emergency accounts off limits. Use a checking account to handle bills. Discipline can also consist of establishing a money market account through an advisor, directly with an investment company or a credit union. Some people find it valuable working with or through an advisor because they will think twice before accessing the dip account. Using an investment company or a credit union creates an extra step to access funds, which can trigger second thoughts regarding the need for the funds. As money market accounts are readily accessible, it is wise to make them less accessible by not allowing check or debit access to the account. To access the account you can call the investment company or your advisor to request a specific dollar amount which can be deposited directly to a bank account, mailed or wired. Other accounts to consider for a dip account, emergency or wealth account are CDs, savings, money market

---

46 CFP Guidelines <www.CFP.net>

accounts with a banking institution or high cash value quality life insurance policies. Keep in mind that some of these accounts have limits on access to funds.

When the primary savings plan is established the secondary savings plan must be implemented. This savings plan considers the future costs, inflation and current fixed interest rates and is based on the year or age you want to have accumulated this wealth. The total sum that is required to have a comfortable or sustainable lifestyle is usually a grand figure. Subsequently, this amount usually knocks people off their feet. The fact is to reach your goals you will have to make concerted efforts to make them a reality. This is why elements four, five and six are so important. Rest assured that by working the plan for abundance, your discretionary income may begin to increase, allowing more opportunities to save and splurge a little.

Financial planning is a continuous process. The objective is to structure your plan in the same way big businesses plan and forecast for a profitable future. In the eyes of the IRS, individuals are like mini enterprises. The more you are able to manage your finances the better you are able to benefit from the system versus being a victim. To further this process, hold the future outcome you envision for you and/or your family in 20 to 30 years and create plans with short-term and medium-term horizons. It is virtually impossible to create a financial plan today to be realized in 30 years and expect the intended outcome to work perfectly. There are far too many variables and unknowns; job security, raises, bonuses, taxes, marriage, divorce, children, aging parents, political changes, inflation, and financial market fluctuations just to name a few. Review long-term plans every 2-3 years like a corporation. This allows you to make adjustments due to guaranteed changes. Throughout every phase you must start from where you are.

The primary savings goal is to save enough to take care of your basic, current and future needs. In other words, it addresses the comfortable lifestyle. Once a comfortable lifestyle is set you can now address the extras, meaning all the things or experiences you would like to have if money were not an issue. To accomplish this goal use discretionary funds, money *not* designated for bills, debt reduction or primary savings, for miscellaneous purchases. This is the extra money that gets spent on the things you can't account for like children asking for money, purchasing the occasional candy bar or magazine. These small purchases add up. By the end of the month we do not realize we have spent $200. Sustainable wealth is about conscientious spending.

Let's look at an example. Say that you have been saving $1,000 per month in a retirement plan and you have 15 years to go before you are officially eligible to retire with maximum benefits. However, the pension income and money from your retirement plan will only grant a survival lifestyle in your retirement years. You realize that if you do not shift gears now you will have an undesirable outcome. So, rather than using that bonus or tax return of $5,000 to add on to the house, you elect to save it in a tax favorable investment that provides competitive, guaranteed rates of return. You also decide that it is time to monetize your hobby, for example, creating unique jewelry designs or making healthy sweets for diabetics. You figure that will generate about $300 per month net after expenses. In addition to increasing your income you take a closer look at your spending and find that you are shelling out about $125 a month on junk. When you add up the amount that could have been saved, it comes to about $10,000 annually. This money needs to flow to an account that is liquid and has a guaranteed outcome. This extra $10,000 and possibly some of the money flowing to the retirement plan must be channeled to a solid financial foundation as illustrated in the *Sustainable Wealth Pyramid* (below).

Once the foundation of your financial house is set, you can steadily build from there into other assets that generate a guaranteed return for retirement. This type of retirement plan resembles the pension plan that used to be the standard retirement package corporations offered employees. Before the emergence of the 401(k) plan in the 1970s, people were able to retire without worry of stock market performance. Plans that provide a guaranteed return with tax benefits will help ensure that you are in a situation where your retirement is a *comfortable lifestyle*. As your income increases from bonuses or cost of living adjustments or as sales grows with your business venture, there is comfort in allocating those earnings into a more aggressive investment. If the investment goes sour, your retirement lifestyle is not compromised. If the investment comes out in your favor, then it is all gravy. This strategy suggests doing almost the opposite of what is commonly advised, which is essentially to put the maximum into your 401(k) plan first and hope the market performs in your favor. Saving for retirement should not be a guessing game. Save for retirement in a way that ensures you will have it when you retire. In some cases contributing the maximum to your 401(k) is efficient and in others it is not. There are strategies that can be employed that mirror the pension plans of the olden days. The types of assets that provide such guarantees are listed in the Financial Foundation and Low Risk section of the Sustainable Wealth Pyramid. Some of the products used to implement the strategies are IRAs, Fixed Annuities and certain types of Life Insurance policies. To design a planning strategy using these products requires a competent financial professional. The point to take away here is that the days of a company providing solid pension plans to all employees that allow the employee to live out their retirement years has waned. The need to change habits to create a comfortable and sustaining lifestyle now and in retirement is more important than ever before.

Element Four: Investing

Investing strategically over a period of time can lead to sustainable wealth. After you have set a solid financial foundation where you have a dip account, emergency and wealth accounts and once you have properly protected your current assets and are funding a retirement plan with guarantees, the next action item is to invest in non-guaranteed assets. The first step when investing is to determine your risk tolerance. How much can you afford to lose? This will often depend on your individual circumstances. The younger you are, the more time you have, the more risk you can afford. However, if you decided to go back to school to get a master's degree and the only real savings you have is your 401(k), it may be advisable to have long-term assets like retirement accounts in a secure fund should you need to tap into it in case of emergencies. Consider personal situations as opposed to following general guidelines. On the other hand, if you follow the plan for abundance, then immediate and short-term needs are met and you are saving medium and long term money in a conservative fashion that can help to ensure you will live with grace and ease. This means, you can take on a bit of risk without worrying if your future needs will be met. The second step is to determine your time horizon. When are you going to need the money? What is it for? Why are you investing? Under what conditions should you buy and/or sell? The third step relates to the profit details. What are the costs? What is the current market condition? What is the desired profit or rate of return? Would a partnership or incorporating be more profitable?

There are multiple ways to create sustainable wealth. The two most popular wealth building strategies are investing in a 401(k) plan and/or buying real estate. The 401(k) plan provides W-2 employees the opportunity to invest money toward their retirement with modest tax benefits for employees with an income of $50,000 or below and a greater benefit to those with an income in excess of $100,000.[47] However, many people don't realize the limitations of a 401(k) plan and the other options available. In a 401(k) plan there are limited funding choices and limited flexibility on your ability to control the funding. Moreover, the government limits the amount you can invest and when you can enter the plan. In addition, 401(k) plans were never designed to be the main source of retirement income for people. Indeed, 401(k) plans have their place with other tax deferred investment vehicles. They pro-

---

[47] Does Participating in a 401(k) Raise Lifetime Taxes? By Jagadeesh Gokhale, Todd Neumann with the Federal Reserve of Cleveland and Laurence J. Kotlikoff from Boston University and the National Bureau of Economic Research

vide an opportunity for people to automatically save pre-tax dollars each time they are paid by an employer. This allows an individual to use a time-tested strategy called dollar cost averaging.[48] When you build sustainable wealth you must be diligent and consistent. Dollar cost averaging creates an opportunity to purchase shares on a regular basis without having to time the market. This allows the investor to purchase shares at a lower price on average over time. As the value of the shares increase over time, that cost per share should ideally be less than the current value. So if you are investing in non-guaranteed assets in a 401(k), 403(b), 457 plans, an IRA or any other tax deferred retirement plan, the plan needs to be supplemented with an additional plan for sustainable wealth that has a guaranteed outcome. The key is to have multiple streams of income that have some degree of asset protection from lawsuits, taxes and divorce.

The other common supplemental investment is in real estate. Real estate offers many benefits such as passive income (cash flow), tax benefits and wealth appreciation. It can also subject one to headaches such as vacancies, maintenance issues, liability concerns and market risk. During the boom of 2005, people felt real estate values could only increase. Well, we know the end to that story. Putting your eggs in one basket is extremely high risk and strongly discouraged. Whatever market you choose to play in, be it stocks, bonds or real estate, it will have its ebbs and flows. It is necessary to educate yourself enough to understand the risks, invest accordingly and have your financial foundation set before you invest in non-guaranteed assets. Clearly, investing provides for greater

---

48 Dollar Cost Averaging is a timing strategy of investing equal dollar amounts regularly and periodically over specific time periods it does not assure a profit against a loss in declining markets. Consider your financial ability and willingness to continue purchases through periods of low price levels.

future outcomes. However, there is an order. The pendulum has shifted to banking on returns versus developing the sustainable wealth building habits. Setting a foundation by funding guaranteed assets and protecting your wealth is imperative to creating sustainable wealth.

Element Five: Tax Strategies[49]

Elements four, five and six happen simultaneously. Implementing a tax strategy is imperative when investing in tangible or intangible assets or a business. Taxes are so intricately woven into different levels of our lives. We are generally taxed on the money we spend on goods by sales tax, investing via capital gains tax, income through state and federal income tax and our total estate in the form of estate tax. Stop and think about the diminishing purchasing power of our money when we have to pay a sales tax on items. Proper tax planning can keep more money in our pockets and under our control. There are legal ways to mitigate sales taxes just as there are benefits to paying taxes. About .50% of the 9.75% CA sales tax goes to public safety and about .25% goes to transportation.[50] Still this regressive tax drags on our purchasing power. When we invest in individual stocks, for example, and we hold the stock for greater than a year, we are taxed at the long-term capital gain rate, which are more favorable than short-term capital rates. Short-term capital gain rates are taxed at ordinary income levels to as much as 45% versus long-term capital gain rates ranging from 0% to 15%.[51]

Owning a business or owning shares of a closely held business provides favorable tax benefits. If you choose to

---

49 PAS and the representative do not provide legal or tax advice or services.
50 California Board of Equalization. *Detailed Description of Sales and Use Tax Rate* available at http://www.boe.ca.gov/news/_sp111500att.html
51 Rates are subject to change in 2010. Available at <http://www.IRS.gov>

own your own business, determining a business entity or type is based on many factors including how the business will be taxed. Many small business owners select a Sub-chapter S corporation instead of a C-corporation because they can avoid the double taxation of the C-corporation. This is often a good place to begin. As your business expands, a C-corporation or an LLC taxed as a C-corporation can provide more financial, business and tax benefits. Owners of C corporations have more flexibility to establish fringe benefit programs for themselves when compared to their counterparts who own interests in pass-through entities such as S corps, LLCs and partnerships. Some fringe benefits are tax favorable and may offset the double taxation, meaning C-corporations are taxed on the corporate level and to the shareholder. This can feel like a double tax if you are the sole owner. Although our tax system is complex, it can work to our personal benefit as well as that of the public. More often people consider the tax implications when they need the money or are ready to sell. Be a Zeallionaire and consider the tax implication before, during and after making financial decisions.

Element Six: Business Enterprise

In this new age, incorporating a business into your financial plan is integral. The profit, appreciation, and tax benefits from a business enterprise are all treated very favorably in the tax codes. Whether you decide to own your own business, become an investor in someone else's business or a limited partner of a business, it is an excellent opportunity for wealth creation. Many lessons can be learned from pursuing a business. Although some people define these lessons as failures, keep the Chinese proverb in mind that states, "Failure is not falling down but refusing to get up." Understand the risks and invest time and money accordingly. It takes fortitude, focus and tenacity and, most of all, belief in one's capabilities to succeed against perceived odds. When starting a business, one factor that is often overlooked are the tax benefits. Choosing the type of entity, whether it is a sole proprietorship, S-corporation or a limited liability corporation has a major effect on how your business will be taxed. A sound tax advisor or CPA can help you decide which entity is best. If you are the independent type, there are online sources to help you decide.

If you are ever faced with an IRS audit, you want to be able to substantiate any deductions or credits you claim. An excellent practice is to keep *all* business related activity and receipts itemized separately from personal activity. This is a common mistake for sole proprietors. Many business expenses are eligible for income tax deductions. Keep good records. Also, be mindful of succession planning in the beginning stages of the business. It is natural not to think of selling your business or transferring it to the next generation when you first open your doors. However, having an idea of how you want your legacy to continue or end will play a major factor in the tax benefits you realize now and in the future. Certain trusts and buy/sell agreements address how and who your businesses can be sold or transferred to with ease. Implementing certain estate planning strategies, like a charitable remainder trusts, can create a charitable deduction and therefore lower your income tax liability now and possible estate tax liability in the future. Planning a smooth transition will create an easier conversion to the intended recipient of the business while making proper provisions for the surviving heirs and/or your favorite non-profit organization.

Element Seven: Regular Monitoring

Everyone that has a goal to create, grow and maintain a solid financial future should have a financial team that monitors wealth regularly. A financial team includes a financial advisor, tax advisor (CPA), attorney(s), banker, loan officer, insurance agent and stock broker. Be in communication with your financial team on a monthly, quarterly or at least annual basis. Note that your tax advisor, financial advisor and estate planning attorney should be acquainted with each other. They are working on your behalf and therefore should communicate with each other to enhance your financial matters. When your needs or goals change your advisory team should be notified. Goals change at various life stages. People get married, divorced, have children, grandchildren, reach college age, retire and change or begin careers. Proper planning requires that you keep your team abreast of these changes to ensure that you stay on track with attaining a solid financial future.

In ever-changing times, Congress sets new rules and regulations related to the financial services industry in almost every session. These changes affect everyone and, if you and your team of advisors[52] are not in the loop, you may not be optimizing your investment power. Monitoring finances and the rules that govern them are integral to creating sustainable wealth.

---

52 Your team of advisors includes your financial advisor, tax advisor (CPA), attorney(s), banker, loan officer, insurance agent and stock broker.

West African Symbol for Faith and Trust in God

Chapter Nine
Motivational Guide

The final stage to creating sustainable wealth is to have tenacity. Many people have been called but few answer. All too often we allow external influences to determine our future. A distinction must be made between possibility and probability. Anything is possible through God that strengthens us. The probability that our vision manifests is reflective of the sum total of our thoughts and subsequent actions that follow. Our present experiences evolve as we focus on the future outcome and release habits that do not support our vision. Creating a spiritual regime to stay on track and motivated will add fuel to reaching our goals. "**Even if you possess desire and discipline, without action you will never attain what you want.**"[53] Belief in self while walking in the footsteps of our Creator is what takes us from a state of procrastination to a state of ACTION. This underlining current of energy is in all of us. Some of us can tap in to it much easier than others, but all of us have the ability to be moved by the Spirit. It calls

---
53 Unknown

forth action. What is your calling? Is it to retire early so that you can have more time with your grandchildren? Are you to create financial freedom so that you can be on the board of many charitable organizations to bring forth change? Or, is your desire to create an eco-friendly business? Whatever your calling is, it is imperative to keep the vision alive and keep your eye on the prize when the road gets rough. Zeallionaires use affirmations, mantras and/or scripture to stay focused and maneuver through tribulations.

The following are a few affirmations to incorporate into our daily lives:

> I AM now connected to the only true source of Infinite Prosperity—GOD, the essence of All That Is. Thank you God for raising my awareness to see the abundant opportunities that are all around me right now. This awareness bestows new vision upon me. This new vision empowers me beyond old fear, doubt, and worry to create a new life of Financial Freedom. I no longer allow any person, thought or event to steal my joy from me. If ever I feel fear, I instantly put my hand on my heart and say, I REMEMBER GOD, CHOOSE LOVE, and CREATE VALUE. Love itself now eliminates all forces that once weakened me. Prosperity Consciousness inspires me to focus solely on creating value for others. Through this value creation, limitless abundance flows to me in the form of money. This reality manifests in harmony with Thy Will for me, Amen.
>
> ~ *Steve D'Annunzio*[54]

---

54 D'Annunzio, Steve. *The Prosperity Paradigm*. Mercury Print. New York. 2006.

ALL ABOUT THE BENJAMINS

Yes, I say yes to the next step in my Spiritual unfoldment.
Today I break all agreements with mediocrity.
I take a stand for excellence in every area of my life.
Sacred power, poise and confidence charge my thoughts, words and activities.
My true nature is abundance and I express it fully.
Gratefully I live these words of truth.
And so it is. Amen.

~ *Michael Bernard Beckwith*[55]

<u>I AM</u>
I AM AWAKENED AWARENESS
I AM THE TRUTH SET FREE
I AM SPIRIT MADE MANIFEST
I AM THE INVITATION ACCEPTED
I AM THE CALL ANSWERED
I AM THE MUSIC
I AM THE DANCE
I AM A [BLACK] WOMAN/[MAN]
SHOWING UP AS
SPIRITUAL, PHYSICAL, EMOTIONAL,
MENTAL & FINANCIAL HEALTH
I AM OUTRAGEOUS & COURAGEOUS SPINNING GOLD
CREATING LEGACIES OF WEALTH

~*Rev. Dr. Queen Adwoa Nyamekye*[56]

The chanting of mantras can center us and help us maintain focus as we make strides toward reaching our intended goal. Mantras are phrases meant to be repeated over and over

---
55 Beckwith, Michael Bernard. *Spiritual Liberation: Fulfilling Your Soul's Potential.* Atria. New York. 2008.
56 Practitioner at Agape International Spiritual Ctr., Culver City, CA

as a gentle reminder of our purpose.[57] They are energy-based sounds that produce physical vibrations.[58] This physical vibration can lead us to action as these sounds develop meaning and intention, resulting in words that have meaning or purpose. For example, the word "hallelujah" evokes a positive vibration and is commonly known as a higher form of praise. Mantras can be used in a number of ways: when used in music they can inspire and, via meditation, create mental stillness. Mantras dig into the subconscious to bring clear thoughts to the consciousness. When practiced regularly and used effectively, mantras meet the needs of our souls and allow for spiritual growth. The repeated phrase should be expressed as if it has already materialized and must focus on what we want as opposed to what we do not want. Ideally we should create our own mantras. The following are examples of the type of messages we should repeat to ourselves when we create mantras:

~Peace and prosperity flow easily and abundantly into my life.
~I am unconditionally loving and supportive.
~I am a listener and a giver.
~God's love is born in my heart and shown in my relationships.
~I am available to be wealthy and be a great blessing to humanity.
~My life is a song of praise and gratitude.
~Hallelujah, Om, hum ma hum ma om (repeat)

---

57 Bartlett, Neal. *Creating Your Own Personal Mantra.* [cited 2008] <http://ezinearticles.com/?Creating-Your-Own-Personal-Mantra&id=897267>
58 Ashley-Farrand, Thomas. <http://www.sanskritmantra.com>

The *Bible*[59] and other sacred texts are great sources for uplifting passages to keep us motivated throughout our lives and at every step of our personal journeys. Listed below are a few verses from the *Bible* that may inspire some of us to take action toward reaching our goals now.

1 Chronicles 4:10-The Jabez Prayer

Oh that you bless me and enlarge my boarder, and that your hand might be with me, and that you would keep me from hurt or harm. And God granted what he asked.

Proverbs 11:25

A generous person will be enriched, and one who gives water will get water.

Ephesians 3:20

God can do immeasurable more than we ask or imagine.

Matthew 7:7-8

Ask, and it shall be given you; search, and you will find; knock, and the door will be opened for you. For everyone who asks receives, and everyone who searches finds, and for everyone who knocks, the door will be opened.

Mark 11:24

So I tell you, whatever you ask for in prayer, believe that you have received it and it shall be yours.

---

[59] *Strong's Exhaustible Concordance* by James Strong is an excellent resource to navigate through the Bible to find scripture that pertains to a particular topic

1 Thessalonians 5:16-18

Rejoice always, pray without ceasing, give thanks in all circumstances; for this is the will of God in Christ Jesus for you.

Isaiah 41:10

So do not fear, for I am with you; do not be dismayed, for I am your God. I will strengthen you and help you; I will uphold you with my righteous right hand."

The journey to creating sustainable wealth in the midst of insanity entails a great deal of patience, determination and internal/external motivation. We must arm ourselves with knowledge in key areas to overcome inevitable challenges as they will arise to test both our commitment and our endurance. It is imperative we surround ourselves with people who support us and our vision. Our social circles must be comprised of people who have the background and resources to help us reach our goals. This group or team will be our support systems when we face the challenges ahead. It is also good to reflect on the intention of our goals whenever we are faced with challenges. The way we deal with these challenges will determine their outcomes. Stay focused and maintain a level of flexibility. Zeallionaires adjust to changes down the line and allow themselves to be led by the Spirit of the living God. Let's agree to make the changes necessary to achieve the lives we deserve. After all, we only have one life to live. Take it on!

Special Acknowledgement

The one person that I can attribute my tenacity to is my grandmother, Carrie Mills. The stories she shared with me throughout the years where packed with sheer determination. Once she was settled on an idea she manifested her vision into reality. I am grateful her blood runs through my veins.

Many people made valuable contributions to this book, both directly and indirectly. And it would not have been complete without the time and thorough work of Albert Neal. His editorial contributions and meticulous attention to detail is appreciated beyond measure. Thank you for the significant amount of time spent in assisting me.

About the Author

Melanie D. Perry is a graduate of the University of California at San Diego where she earned a Bachelor of Science degree in Quantitative Economics. As a CERTIFIED FINANCIAL PLANNER™ candidate, Perry has partnered with Pacific Advisors where she specializes in tax efficient strategies that increase wealth and establish legacies. She has helped numerous clients retire comfortably, send children to college and protect themselves from financial ruin.

Perry is committed to educating people on financial matters and has conducted numerous financial literacy seminars and workshops for organizations throughout the country. She hosted the radio show, "Getting Your Financial House in Order" and can be heard on the KPFK radio program "Some of Us Are Brave" where she delivers financial tips to audiences across the nation. Perry's goal is to share her financial knowledge and lead people to wealth by awakening the desire to live truly abundant lives NOW.

Melanie Perry, Registered Representative of Park Avenue Securities, LLC (PAS), 1550 W. Colorado Blvd., Pasadena, CA 91105, 1.323.255.8800. Securities products and services are offered through PAS, a registered broker/dealer. Financial Professional, The Guardian Life Insurance Company of America (Guardian), New York, NY PAS is an indirect, wholly owned subsidiary of Guardian. Pacific Advisors, Inc. is not an affiliate or subsidiary of PAS or Guardian. Insurance Products offered through Pacific Regional Insurance Services, a DBA of Pacific Advisors, Inc. Pacific Advisors, Inc. is not an independent registered investment advisor. California Insurance License # 0C86870; CA.

Neither Park Avenue Securities, Guardian, nor their representatives render legal or tax advice. Please consult with your attorney, accountant, and/or tax advisor for advice concerning your particular circumstances.

Appendix:

BALANCE SHEET

Assets   -   Liabilities

PERSONAL PROPERTY
SAVINGS
INVESTMENTS
RETIREMENT
REAL ESTATE
BUSINESS

TAXES
SHORT TERM DEBT
MORTGAGES
BUSINESS DEBT

= **Net worth**

Statement of Cash Flow

	January	February
INFLOWS:		
Main Salary	-------------	-------------
Dividend Income	-------------	-------------
Interest Income	-------------	-------------
1099 Income	-------------	-------------
Business Income	-------------	-------------
Rental Income	-------------	-------------
Sub Total		
OUTFLOWS:		
Savings & Investment	-------------	-------------
Retirement Savings	-------------	-------------
Dividends	-------------	-------------
Interest	-------------	-------------
Sub Total		
FIXED OUTFLOWS		
Rent/Mortgage	-------------	-------------
Property Taxes	-------------	-------------
Hm.owners/Renter's Ins.	-------------	-------------
Utilities	-------------	-------------
Telephone	-------------	-------------
Auto Payment	-------------	-------------
Auto Insurance	-------------	-------------
Gas/Oil/Maintenance	-------------	-------------
Debt Payments	-------------	-------------
Sub Total		

	January	February
VARIABLE OUTFLOWS	----------------	----------------
Taxes*	----------------	----------------
Food	----------------	----------------
Medical/Dental	----------------	----------------
Clothing/Personal Care	----------------	----------------
Child Care	----------------	----------------
Entertainment/Vacation	----------------	----------------
Discretionary	----------------	----------------
Sub Total	----------------	----------------
Sub Totals of Inflows	----------------	----------------
Sub Total of Outflows	----------------	----------------
Net Cash Flow	----------------	----------------
(+/-) Cash Flows		
*Note the Taxes:	----------------	----------------
FICA/MED	----------------	----------------
SDI Tax	----------------	----------------
Estimated Payments	----------------	----------------
Federal Withholdings	----------------	----------------
TOTAL	----------------	----------------

Accounting for your monthly expenses marks the behavior of a Zeallionaire™.

Dumping Debt: Fast and Easy

STEP ONE: List all of your consumer debt using the following chart. This includes credit cards, charge accounts, and any high-interest loans that are not against assets and other liabilities. In order to efficiently keep track, be sure to organize your payments electronically.

	Name of Creditor	Amount Owned	Minimum Payment	Interest Rate	Factoring Number
1	Personal Credit Card A	$5,200.00	$120.00	7.99%	44
2	Business Credit Card	$4,800.00	$95.00	8.24%	50
3	Line of Credit	$16,900.00	$70.00	5.13%	241
4	Personal Credit Card B	$3,600.00	$65.00	8.99%	55

Calculating the Factoring Number

STEP TWO: Take the amount owed and divide it by the minimum payment required. As illustrated above.

Order of Priority Payoff

STEP THREE: Find the debt with the lowest factoring number and place it at the top of the list. You want to pay this debt off first. Place the remaining debt in increasing order, where the factoring numbers flows from smallest to largest.

	Name of Creditor	Factoring Number	Minimum Payment
1	Personal Credit Card A	44	$120.00
2	Business Credit Card	50	$95.00
3	Personal Credit Card B	55	$65.00
4	Line of Credit	241	$70.00
		Total	$350.00

Accelerate the elimination of debt

STEP FOUR: Create a cash flow statement so that you have a clear understanding of where your money is coming from and where it is going. This will help you find the funds to eliminate debt at a faster rate. You need to find at least $100.00 and at best $200.00 to dump the debt. This may sound like a lot of money, however when it is broken down it is only about $3.00 to $7.00 per day. Think of the daily coffee or the fast food you buy. Incorporating wealthy habits by reducing consumption and taking control of your finances will lead to creating sustainable wealth.

Dumping unsecured debt for good

STEP FIVE: In our example, your total payment is $550 ($350 + $200). Once you have paid off the first debt ($320 = $120 + $200) you are ready to tackle the next one. Try to refrain from spending that money. You now have $320 to add to the next minimum payment of $95, for a total of $415. Continue with this strategy until you have completely dumped your debt. It is imperative to save and dump debt at the same time. If the debt payment is $550 then save $550. If that is too steep, save at least $3.00 a day. Once you have eliminated the debt, add these payments to your savings. Maintain the habit of saving to use cash to buy consumables and handle emergencies verses racking up debt. A suggested cushion is to have one month of your gross income in your dip account, an emergency account with three to twelve months of your expenses (at least) and a wealth account to buy assets. A habit of saving and using helps to create sustainable wealth.

Melanie Perry

Financial Advisor
Pacific Advisors, LLC
1550 W. Colorado Blvd.
Pasadena, CA 91105
323.258.5053

Givers Gain

Give a gift that keeps on giving. Financial empowerment is void in many communities. Knowledge, planning and tenacity are the critical components that produce Zeallionaires.

Contributing the financial well-being of others through education is priceless.

To order this book please visit www.AATBonline.com
Or call
877.907.AATB

www.ingramcontent.com/pod-product-compliance
Lightning Source LLC
Chambersburg PA
CBHW031554300426
44111CB00006BA/317